I0010211

Continuous Innovation

How successful organizations
continuously develop, scale, and
embed innovations to lead
tomorrow's markets

http://www.continuousinnovation.net

Arent van 't Spijker

Technics Publications

Published by:

2 Lindsley Road
Basking Ridge, NJ 07920 USA

https://www.TechnicsPub.com

Edited by Lauren McCafferty
Cover design by Lorena Molinari

First Printing 2019
Copyright © 2019 by Arent van 't Spijker

ISBN, print ed.	9781634625623
ISBN, Kindle ed.	9781634625630
ISBN, ePub ed.	9781634625647
ISBN, PDF ed.	9781634625654

Library of Congress Control Number: 2019947022.

Contents

"In 2008, 25 percent of the company's revenue came from products created in the last five years. Today, that number is 34 percent. We are $30 billion in terms of revenue as a company, meaning over $10 billion of the products we are selling today did not exist five years ago. In 2017, we expect that number to be 40%."

Inge Thulin, President and CEO of 3M in 2013

About this Book

When I started writing this book, I was looking for a way to structure my thoughts on why so many of my corporate clients struggled with being consistent in their innovation efforts. Writing the book not only helped me to structure my thoughts, it led to many pleasant and insightful discussions with inspiring people. I found that writing, like innovation, is about exchanging ideas and experiences and building upon them.

My gratitude goes to those people who have helped me to structure my ideas. To those who disagreed, who prompted me to 'kill my darlings' and who brought me fresh perspectives. I would like to thank the many brilliant people at BlinkLane Consulting and Gladwell Academy for their support in shaping the Continuous Innovation Framework. And the many colleagues and friends who helped me in writing this book. In particular, thanks to Ed Peelen at the University of Amsterdam for pointing out scientific relevance, and Arjen Eriks at Schuberg Philis for bringing business focus in combination with amazing places to have discussions. And Cor Nagtegaal, whose dedication and in-depth analysis of the book has provided valuable structure, focus, and visualization.

This book is about the great ideas that are produced by people in business and technology. Having such ideas is not anyone's prerogative. Great ideas are not exclusive to the brilliant minds. They are not exclusively for inventors, technicians, or teachers. Not for PhDs or high school dropouts. Not for managers or entrepreneurs. Not for men or women. This book acknowledges everyone's abilities and skills when demonstrated. Having said this, for simplicity and clarity, I refer to the masculine-form when providing examples or explanations.

CHAPTER 1
The Times are Changing

Incumbents do not win because they are big

On February 13, 1888, London was bustling with positive energy. The *London City*, the capital's financial district, formed the heart of international finance and was at the height of its importance. Capitalizing on the atmosphere of success and entrepreneurship, two young men, Douglas MacRae and Horatio Bottomly had joined in a business venture and founded a financial newspaper entitled 'The Financial Times.' The new publication claimed to be *'Without Fear and Without Favour'* and promoted itself as *'the friend of The Honest Financier and The Respectable Broker, and the enemy of The*

Unprincipled Promoter and The Gambling Operator.' The four-page newspaper quickly established its reputation as an independent and respectable commentary on the stock exchange and circulation started to grow. But Bottomly, an avid trader himself, frequently used The Financial Times to promote fictitious stories that boosted the market price of stocks that he intended to sell and undermined the value of those he was trying to buy. Less than a year after their joint venture, MacRae had had enough, broke off relations with Bottomly and continued the Financial Times by himself.

From then on, the lives of the two men could not have drifted further apart. Bottomly turned into a shady politician, was put on trial for fraud, managed to escape conviction, and ultimately made a fortune during the infamous 'Kaffir boom' in African gold mining shares. Before the turn of the century, the friend of The Honest Financier and the enemy of The Unprincipled Promoter had become a fraudster and trader in shady shares, albeit a very famous and wealthy one.

MacRae, eventually, would equally strike good fortune and fame, but for him, it was based on hard and honest labor and a stroke of genius that is famous to this very day. In 1893, while in severe competition with the *Financial News*, MacRae was desperate to find a way to distinguish the Financial Times from its rival. Reputation, independence, and quality had kept the publication alive, but nowhere near hegemonic. A drastic change was needed to place the Financial Times firmly in the lead.

In January 1893, MacRae decided to start printing the Financial Times on pink paper. The decision resonates to this day as across the globe the Financial Times still stands out in newsstands and as a leading example in marketing innovation taught in business schools across the world. According to popular business literature, McRae chose the color to make the publication instantly recognizable on the newsstands, but the pink color had an important side effect. The pink coloring was achieved by using less bleach in the manufacturing of the paper. This not only colored the paper but actually made the paper cheaper. MacRae never publicly disclosed his reasons for choosing to print on colored paper, so it is not unthinkable that one of the greatest marketing innovations in history was actually a cost-saving measure.

The recognizable pink proved to be a great driver for success and when in 1895 the 'Kaffir boom' lead to hectic scenes on the London Stock Exchange (and to great fortune for Horatio Bottomly), the Financial Times was recognizably in the right place at the right time. The rapid increase in readership and advertising provided the opportunity to demonstrate its independence and respectable commentary to a large audience and settled its reputation as the leading source of financial information *Without Fear and Without Favour.*' And with it settled its long-term business future.

Innovative, yet reluctant to change

MacRae set the standard for innovation early in the history of the Financial Times. Pink paper was probably not the first, and most certainly not the last, innovation in the history of the company. While remaining steadfast in quality and independent reporting,

MacRae was always quick to implement new technology, such as the Linotype machine, which greatly reduced labor costs as it replaced traditional manual typesetters. Apart from saving time, the Linotype machine brought a crisp, fresh typeface to the paper, adding to the appearance of quality of the publication.

Between the turn of the century and the second world war, innovation at the Financial Times became engrained in its culture and was never limited to technological innovation. Between 1945 and 1990, its peers repeatedly praised the Financial Times for its advances in areas such as graphic design, marketing, and editorial scope. In the 1960s, the newspaper was the first to introduce a *Technology* section. From the early 1970s it placed specific focus on Europe as an economic region. Subscription rates proved that the course the Financial Times was sailing was the right one. In 1960, circulation reached 130,000. In the early 1980s that figure had grown to 250,000 and by the turn of the 20th century, it had reached 450,000.

True to character, the Financial Times was an early adopter of digital technology. As early as 1995, one year after the world wide web was created, the *Financial Times* launched its website at FT.com. Little did the company realize then that this very world wide web would become one of the biggest challenges in its hundred-year history.

Despite its 'innovative' approach, the one thing that had not changed over the years was the newspaper itself. A century after its inception, The Financial Times was still a newspaper reporting on the wellbeing of stock markets and trade. Sure, the paper was pinkish – an innovation in the way paper was produced. It also set trends in graphic design and pioneered new methods to market financial news. Yet the Financial Times as a concept – the newspaper itself – had proven to be quite reluctant to change. For decades, such steadfastness had been a driver for success. During two world wars and many more economic crises, the paper had stood tall. But the Internet, supported by an army of eager, bright entrepreneurial minds, was going to change all that.

Competition from technology

For Nathan Richardson, a graduate from Georgetown University and at the time in his mid-twenties, the launch of FT.com must have seemed anything but innovative. Between 1994 and 1998, Richardson had already lived and worked in London, Turkey, Warsaw, Saudi Arabia, and South Africa as a management trainee for Citibank. He had, however, no intention to get stuck in corporate life on a salary and an (admittedly tantalizing) bonus. Instead, Richardson was ready to dive head-first into the Internet startup bonanza, change corporate finance from the ground up, risk all and become a millionaire while doing it. Richardson teamed with startup veterans Michael Baum and Robert Simon to form dotBank, an online payment platform and a key competitor to PayPal at the time. In 2000, at the height of the dotcom bubble and while in fierce competition with Elon Musk at PayPal, dotBank was acquired by Yahoo! for no less than US$100 million. As part of the deal, Richardson went to work for Yahoo! Within a few months, he was asked by the management of Yahoo! to form a new startup, that would become the single biggest threat to The Wall Street Journal and

The Financial Times. The new startup was called *Yahoo! Finance*.

Yahoo Finance started out as a simple portal providing online news for traders and financial enthusiasts. The site was anything but out of the ordinary. Just like any other financial publication, it used the Reuters stock price ticker and it featured financial articles from various third-party sources. The news was displayed in an easy to read format, with a search bar and categories for specific areas of interest. Yahoo! Finance was, with respect, an online copy of the Financial Times' concept, but without their professional editorial board and century of experience.

Obviously, when Richardson started competing, he was not going to aim for the unique selling points of the Wall Street Journal and The Financial Times. Instead, he turned to his own expertise: data analytics. *Yahoo! Finance* decided to not play editor and 'decide' what people wanted to read but instead measured what people were actually reading during their visits. Each day, Richardson and his team would analyze the usage patterns of visitors and determine what worked and what did not.

Using streams of data from clicks and page views, the Yahoo! Finance team built an intricate map of people's likes, dislikes, and behavior and used that information to build a personalized portal that attracted people to read more pages. Once inside, they used data to make the site more 'sticky' - to keep people on the site longer. By analyzing traffic on the site, Richardson and his team discovered that readers were more interested in 'optimizing tax returns' and 'credit management' than in 'university savings' and 'links to online tools for preparing taxes.' Before long, the number of content partners grew from 10 to over 200 and Richardson and his team were competing head-on with the Wall Street Journal and the Financial Times. Not because they were trying to be a better newspaper but because they were definitely better data scientists.

Within months after launching, *Yahoo! Finance* started to outpace the incumbent players in the market in terms of unique visitors, return visits, and thus online advertising revenues. Adding to the destructive power, the team started applying the same analytical capability to target advertisements at specific audiences. Based on a visitor's preferences and click patterns, banner ads would be targeted only at individuals with specific behavior matching the advertisers' message. This allowed Yahoo! Finance to earn a premium price for its ad placements, and revenue grew accordingly, at the expense of its competitors. Incumbent players responded in much the same way that they had been doing for decades: they emphasized their own quality over Yahoo!'s and offered discounts on cost per mille (CPM), the price per 1,000 viewed ad banners.

All too quickly, it became clear that where FT.com viewed itself as a quality financial newspaper which offered the option to advertise in the margin of its content, Yahoo! Finance regarded itself a lead-generator for advertisers which used financial content to analyze and determine the quality of the leads. Advertisers were quick to discover that Yahoo!'s proposition was favorable.

Adding insult to injury, Richardson and his team concluded that they could vastly improve on the portal's stock ticker that was supplied by Reuters. The stock ticker attracted many visitors to the site but was out of Yahoo!'s control. In the most startup of ways, Richardson opened an office in India, hired six developers, pulled together financial market data and ticker feeds and created Yahoo!'s own stock ticker quote box. The box was made in such a way that third party website owners could publish it on their websites and (because it was clickable), direct traffic straight to the Yahoo! Site and earn a referral fee. With early help of sites such as Motley Fool and Quicken, Yahoo! Finance saw a massive increase in traffic towards its site, and thus to its advertisers. It was a key driver in the success that grew the business from a revenue of US$10 million in 2000 to US$110 million only 5 years later. The innovation power of a single startup had begun to seriously wreak havoc on the former innovation champion, which had forgotten to innovate its core business.

Bowler hats and hoodies

By 2006, the proverbial excrement had come into contact with the ventilator at The Financial Times (FT). In just five years, advertising income had dropped by almost 25%. Traditionally, advertising had generated three-quarters of the annual income, now it was down to half. Subscription rates were also dropping dramatically, giving way to free online financial news. The epitome of the British banker in pin-striped suit and bowler hat had been surpassed by a whiz kid with a laptop in a hoodie.

To John Ridding (the newly-appointed CEO of the Financial Times) and Lionel Barber (who had been the Editor for less than a year), it was clear that a radical change was required to turn the tide. In July 2006, the board announced the "New Newsroom" project, with the aim to integrate the print publication more closely with its online presence and in the process cut 10% of the editorial staff. Although criticized by many as a traditional 'laying off' response to digital disruption, the decision made more than just economic sense. The project heralded the first significant attempt to innovate 'the newspaper' itself. The Financial Times were changing.

The change that Ridding set out to achieve would mark not only a turning point for the paper but would become an example of how incumbent businesses can turn digital disruption into a competitive advantage against its very disruptors. To do so, the Financial Times would have to do more than generate more traffic than Yahoo! It would have to innovate its way out of trouble.

In 2007, the FT.com was the first newspaper to implement a metered paywall, a system in which online readers are allowed to read a certain number of articles on the site for free, and then requires them to pay. The move was controversial and was fiercely debated. Many viewed the paywall as a sign that the Financial Times was stuck in old-fashioned methods. After all, the Internet offered all content for free. Why would anyone want to pay for articles on FT.com when Yahoo! Finance offered them at no cost? But in the mind of Ridding, the paywall was not designed to keep non-paying readers away from FT.com, it was a great way to get new, loyal customers in. By signing up for metered access, readers provided FT.com with valuable personal data and an exceptional mechanism to track their personal behavior and interests that far outweighed Yahoo!'s clickstream data.

FT.com did not abuse the data to spam the user with advertisements, instead, they identified detailed interests and preferences and provided unrivaled relevant content from its unique editorial staff. In much greater detail and with more trust than any Yahoo!-like competitor could offer. Within 5 years, FT.com had attracted 5 million registrants who had provided their names, addresses, job responsibility, job title, and industry. The FT.com team could now target marketing messages and newsletters at specific interest groups, with their explicit permission. By collecting data from its registrants, FT.com proved it could be more relevant to its readers. First-class content, at the core of the very being of the company, combined with targeted relevance resulted in a formidable conversion from (free) metered users to paying digital subscribers.

In addition, by using the data provided by its readers, FT.com could offer advertisers the chance to advertise only with readers from specific industries or with specific functions. At a premium price, of course. Today, FT.com offers advertisers a dashboard, called Deep View, displaying the exact results of each ad in each campaign. In an interview on Mashable.com, Ridding mentioned, "We can prove in real-time quite effectively what advertising is working and put that data in front of advertisers. Marketers have to justify every cent of what [they're] spending. Our job is to provide the tools and information to justify that decision for running a campaign with the FT rather than anyone else." (Indvik, 2013)

In an ad-market that has declined 75% in 10 years' time (from US$49 million in 2005 to US$12 million in 2016), such tools and information make the difference between being in or out of business. In an interview in The Media Briefing, Ridding explained: "We've seen year after year of often pretty chunky decline in ads, which for most of that 125 years has been our single biggest source of revenue. [...] We've been trying to build the new while managing the decline of the legacy. That's been tough from a profit perspective, but now we've achieved critical mass in digital and the subscriptions." (Jackson, 2014)

Even in a market of flattening revenues, FT Group has shown an underlying profit growth of 17 percent year on year. Ten years after the initial disruption by technology startups, the century worth of experience, reputation and reader-focus once again paid off. In the early years of the Internet, FT.com struggled to see a difference between its core product, its distribution media, and its business model. Now it has gained experience in new technologies, their quirks and merits and has learned to apply them to its core strengths: superior quality editorial content, reputation and, again, innovation. After 10 years, the pink incumbent had beaten its disruptor at its own game.

CHAPTER 2
Why You Should Read
This Book

We tend to underestimate the effect of
technology in the long run

The 21st-century paradigm of 'young angry' startups leapfrogging 'old and sedated' incumbents by using innovative, digital technology is shifting. Not just because incumbents have mastered the art of Lean Startup methodologies and have now become as fast and nimble in developing breakthrough tech. Indeed, almost a decade after Eric Ries published his book '*The Lean Startup*,' most incumbents have experimented with short-cycled development of innovations, innovation labs, and 'corporate garages.' But the shift is neither in the technology nor in the methodology. Rather it is in the fact that the raw material required to add value to any product or service, data, has become available to almost anyone at almost any time.

Data fuels digital technology with the power to provide real-time functionality. If digital technology brought us news apps, data brought us personalized news. If digital technology brought us satellite navigation, data brought us real-time traffic updates and rerouting. If digital technology brought us self-learning algorithms, data brought us Artificial Intelligence. Where digital technology enables innovation, data accelerates it. Exactly this acceleration is what renders innovation cycles omnipresent and relentless.

The impact of data on our environment, or 'datafication'[1], as we will call it in this book, didn't just appear out of nowhere. It is a logical consequence of developments that started as early as the 1980s. However, only over the last few years have we begun to see its impact on business.

One thing is certain: data-driven, digital innovation is increasing in speed dramatically and its impact on people and businesses is bigger than ever before. This book is not a Nostradamian prediction of where digital technology and data will take us in the next decades. Apart from being quite useless in the past, such

---

[1] The term 'datafication' was first introduced by Viktor Mayer-Schoenberger and Kenneth Cukier in their book Big Data, A Revolution That Will Transform the Way We Live Work and Think (Mayer-Schoenberger, 2013).

predictions have almost always proven to be subject to Amara's law which states that "we tend to overestimate the effect of a technology in the short run and underestimate the effect in the long run." More importantly, I do not believe that *technology* will take us anywhere. I believe that *people* take us places; technology and data merely enable them in ever more creative ways to set things in motion. This motion is what we call innovation.

There is a rather awkward way in which digital technology proponents tend to claim the term 'technology' to describe their own niche while carelessly bypassing an equally awe-inspiring range of technologies that are not all digital, including nanotech, rocketry, biotechnology, and pharmaceutics. Having said this, I feel the need to point out that I too, for reasons of simplicity and without any claim to exclusivity, use the term 'technology' to describe what are predominantly digital technologies, yet without putting this digital technology itself on a pedestal.

Many people aligned with the 'Singularity' movement, including digital technology gurus like Kevin Kelly and Ray Kurzweil, seem to believe that digital technology has a mind of its own (Kelly, 2010) or will outsmart humanity all by itself (Kurzweil, 2005). On the contrary, I believe that for the next few decades, at least, digital technology will serve as an expansive and sophisticated toolkit. I believe it is not the technology, but the *availability* of technology to enthusiasts, entrepreneurs, and corporations that will drive innovation. I believe the availability of technology will affect governments, organizations, individuals, and society as a whole.

Rather than a digital technology-centric prediction of the future, this book is about how today, all around us, people and organizations are confronted by digital technological developments, driven by, and adding to, the widespread availability and exchange of data. Independently of one another, they increase the joint speed of developments. Global data-driven innovation throttles up development to the extent where innovation is the status quo rather than the 'agent for continuous disruptive change.' This development affects every organization at every level.

This book is about getting ahead in times of continuous change. About understanding how the widespread availability of technology and data changes your business environment and why your organization needs to change with it. It is about how you should assess your organization's position in the marketplace and about how to set a direction in which to adapt to the changes taking place and those that lie ahead. Most of all, it seeks to inspire you to find the opportunities for your organization to effectively use digital technology to deliver tangible value to your customers.

The book is structured into three sections. In Part I, *Creative destruction and disruptive innovation*, I will explain why and how digital technology, and data, in particular, is generating unprecedented impact now, and why this creates a new competitive landscape in businesses of all sizes and in all industries. In Part II, *Three Plateaus of Innovation Strategy*, I present a model for assessing the capabilities and position of your organization in the new business landscape and that helps you determine a roadmap for growth. Finally, in Part III,

Creating Continuity, I will address the new rules for organizational design and key success factors of moving through the three plateaus and creating an organizational model to allow for continuous innovation.

PART I
Creative Destruction and Disruptive Innovation

CHAPTER 3
The Increasing Speed
of Disruption

How digital technology creates
inferior solutions faster

I n the early hours of January 8th, 1950, Joseph Alois Schumpeter died at the age of 66. He died a peaceful death, in his bed after an evening of work on economic theory. The last thing he did was read from Euridipes' plays, in the original Greek. On this morning, the world lost one of the most remarkable and influential economists, whose theories on innovation and disruption would not be seriously challenged or refined for another 45 years and which are still part of the foundation of modern business science. The peace in which he died stood in stark contrast to the turmoil he had seen in his life. Schumpeter, born in a middle-class family in what is today the Czech Republic, was a compelling man who both appeared and behaved as an aristocrat. As an academic, he was as flamboyant as he was brilliant, and his early life was a far cry from a steady, predictable academic career.

In 1912, after publishing his first economic theory, *The History of Economic Development,* Schumpeter embarked on an exuberant decade in which he practiced law in Cairo, served as an Egyptian princess' private banker, and went on to become Austria's first republican Minister of Finance in 1919. A few years later Schumpeter gained great fortune as a banker, only to go bankrupt in the 1924 Vienna stock market crash. It marked a turning point in his fortune. In 1926, the flamboyant Schumpeter lost his mother and, two months later, his wife and newborn son.

Heartbroken and almost penniless, Schumpeter returned to academic life and eventually moved to the United States to work and teach at Harvard. Only there did he gain the status and recognition as an economist he had coveted for so long. A recognition he held alongside his ongoing reputation as a flamboyant aristocrat. Schumpeter's status and lifestyle are probably best remembered in his own account of his ambitions: "I strive to become the world's greatest lover, greatest horseman, and greatest economist. Alas," he would then say with a mischievous smile, "things are not going well with the horses."

Schumpeter's creative destruction

Most of the work of Joseph Schumpeter is based on his early work, 'Business Cycles', published in 1939. In this book, he firmly established the idea that the economy consists of cycles, in which the existing market, or cycle, is dominated by systems that seek protection of assets and optimization of resources. Each cycle is inevitably disrupted by entrepreneurs (as opposed to incumbent firms) who seek profits outside the convention-bound circular flow. They do so through the introduction of new products, production techniques, logistics, and organizational forms.

Entrepreneurs, Schumpeter claims, 'raid' existing resources from the incumbent firms and divert them to their innovative uses, thereby creating instability in the circular flow. They 'leapfrog' over the incumbents and take center stage. The market consequently absorbs the new in favor of the old in a process of 'Creative Destruction.' From his 1942 publication: "Those revolutions are not strictly incessant; they occur in discrete rushes which are separated from each other by spans of comparative quiet. The process as a whole works incessantly however, in the sense that there always is either revolution or absorption of the results of revolution, both together forming what is known as business cycles." (Schumpeter, 1942) Although Schumpeter does not stipulate an exact or even an average duration of a cycle, in his later work he estimates that a typical business cycle may last between 7 and 11 years.

Schumpeter's ideas on innovation have become the norm for how most people view the subject. Innovation happens in continuous fluctuations between the destruction of existing products by innovative new ones, the following solidification of these innovations, and the destruction of them in the beginning of a new cycle.

During the solidification phase, Schumpeter expects entrepreneurs to become frustrated enough by the existing offerings and their lack of improvement to dare to introduce new solutions into the market in order to capture a piece of the market. Innovation thus is not a continuous process, but rather a wave-like process, because innovations need time to solidify and become the new norm before a new wave could break.

In addition, Schumpeter dubbed entrepreneurs on the supply side to be the driving force behind innovation, instead of the customers on the demand side. This idea further strengthens the wave-analogy because customer demand would most likely be aimed at incumbents and stimulate them to *improve* their offering, rather than radically innovate, so as not to break the solid base. By not creating entirely new solutions, the market pushes forward latent demand into a wave that requires only minimal entrepreneurial push to break into 'creative destruction.'

Christensen's disruptive innovation

Fifty years after Schumpeter, American scientist Clayton Christensen explained in vivid detail *why* incumbents would, time and again, be surprised by the crashing waves of creative destruction. In 1995, Clayton Christensen wrote an influential article in Harvard Business Review, entitled 'Disruptive Technologies Catching the Wave'. (Christensen, 1995).

In this article, he coined the term 'disruptive innovation' to describe a situation in which companies that offer new, seemingly inferior solutions quickly gain market share from incumbent businesses, disrupting the status quo of the market. Working from the ideas in his article and scholarly work, Christensen went on to become the world's leading thinker on industry disruption. In the words of Christensen, disruption is a process in which "a smaller company with fewer resources is able to successfully challenge established incumbent businesses." (Christensen, What is Disruptive Innovation, 2015)

Disruption happens when incumbent businesses, while focusing on their top clientele, overlook the needs of less profitable segments. New entrants seize the opportunity to serve these segments, usually with different technology and functionality and almost always at a lower price. Incumbents tend to ignore these 'inferior solutions' arguing that their customers have no need for a cheap substitute. The disruptors, when growing their business, are then able to improve the quality of their products and service levels to the point where they become competitive with the incumbents' offerings, while preserving the advantages that drove their initial success. When incumbents' customers start to switch sides in larger number, disruption has occurred. The disruptor has 'leapfrogged' the incumbent and disruptive innovation is a fact.

The mechanism of disruption is quite similar to what Schumpeter described fifty years earlier as 'gales of creative destruction' with two major differences: First, Christensen's disruptors tend not to 'raid' incumbent's resources by offering better products, but increase pressure in the market by 'side-tracking' the existing market with inferior offerings. Second, and perhaps more significant in its impact, Christensen expects his disruptive innovations to take place not in Schumpeter's 7 to 11-year span of a business cycle, but in cycles of no more than five years.

Continuous innovation

Today, the concept of disruptive innovation has acquired another level of complexity, along with operating at an even higher speed. Up until the last few years, disruptive innovation was primarily related to, and instigated by, technological development that replaced existing offerings in an existing market. A classic example of this is the demise of the leading position in telegraphy of Western Union. The company miscalculated the relevance of telephony as a threat to telegraphy, declined to acquire Bell's patents for the telephone for US$100,000 (Lapsley, 2011), and quickly lost its core business to the rising success of the telephone.

Procter & Gamble demonstrated the flipside of the coin with its surprise takeover of the teeth whitening market when it took on the existing US$500 million professional dentists' market with a US$44 product called *Crest Whitestrips*. Not only did the product generate US$200 million in turnover, it quadrupled the market for tooth whitening products. (Bielaszka-DuVernay, 2009)

Today disruptive innovation tends to be identified with small startup companies that use relatively new technology to create novel solutions to problems. Not only do these companies frequently lack the resources and scale to create a high quality, widely marketed product from the start, they also tend to build on experimental, unproven technology. This does not mean that their products are bad or unattractive, on the contrary. But both factors mean that their products are not suited for a large market and high-volume distribution.

However, when their innovative base technology becomes more mainstream and initial business success or venture capital allows the startup company to scale, the company can quickly take market share from incumbents with a superior and often cheaper product. So far, this story conforms to Christensen's theory. Indeed, in business media, blogs, articles, and books, the term *disruptive innovation* has become increasingly synonymous with terms like 'digital technology' and 'startups.' Companies like Uber and AirBnB are labeled 'disruptive' to the taxi-industry and the hotel business.

But no one other than Christensen himself took a stance against this popular train of thought, arguing that (oversimplifying his argument) disruptive innovation is about gradually causing an irreversible shift in market balance by nibbling away market share at the edges of an incumbent's business. It happens through offering inferior solutions to niche customer segments, not by using innovative technology to offer superior products to "bread-and-butter customers." (Christensen, What is Disruptive Innovation, 2015)

Christensen states that most high-tech startups do not actually 'disrupt' their incumbent counterparts. They 'merely' create more advanced digital alternatives to the existing offerings and then use digital technology's characteristics to expand the core products' breadth of service. Uber, from the start, offered a service superior to that of its incumbent opponents: easy hailing of a ride, cashless payment, great reliability, and competitive pricing. It caused incumbents to respond immediately, creating their own hailing apps and payment systems. Uber did not *disrupt* the taxi market, Christensen stated, it *shifted its focus*.

I believe that Christensen is semantically correct. However, I also believe that since 1995 the innovation landscape has witnessed the addition of a new dimension which causes great industry disruption: speed. Earlier on, incumbents were primarily taken by surprise by inferior solutions rising to unexpected success to take market share away from them. Even when they could have seen the disruptors coming from afar, they would not have recognized them as potential threats.

Today, the surprise, and with it the disruption is caused by the sheer speed at which digital technology allows new entrants to create and market new, superior offerings and with them surprise and overwhelm incumbents. Digital technology has created a competitive landscape in which business cycles no longer last 7 to 11 years, not even five years, but have shrunk to the duration of a hackathon. If twenty-five years ago 'gales of creative destruction' gave way to 'disruptive innovation' then today, disruptive innovation gives way to *continuous innovation*.

Innovation self-assessment

To assess the innovative position of your own organization, you can perform a simple exercise. In it, you will plot two or three recently launched digital products or services in a matrix. The exercise is both interesting and fun because, as you read along, this book will explain by the positioning you make here, how innovative your organization really is. And you may recognize some of the difficulties or success factors your organization may have encountered while introducing the innovations into the market.

First, take a sheet of blank paper and draw a simple matrix. The horizontal axis describes the organization and market. On its far left are your current organization and the markets it serves. The further to the right you go, the further you move away from the comfort of your current organization. The vertical axis describes the technology and its exploitation. At the bottom of the axis is the technology your organization currently uses and is very familiar with. The further to the top you go, the more exotic the technology is to your organization and thus the more difficult to implement and use.

Now, take your own organization's capabilities, resources, and activities as a starting point and for two recently launched digital products or services in your organization, ask yourself the following questions:

Was the technology needed for the innovation familiar to your organization and within your organization's comfort zone to use or operate? Or was your organization very inexperienced with this kind of technology, its implementation, or operation? Plot your position on the vertical axis, where the bottom of the axis represents the answer 'we are experienced and familiar with this technology' and the top of the axis represents 'we are highly uncertain about this technology.'

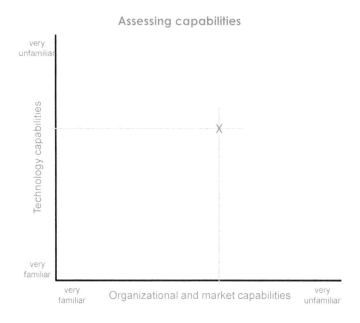

Is the market you are going to serve an existing customer base or a market that you already serve? Or is it a market you are not familiar with or for which you lack the right type of organization? Plot your position on the horizontal axis, where the left of the axis represents the answer 'we are familiar in this market and well organized and equipped to service it.' The right side of the axis represents 'we are highly uncertain about this market and not very well organized to service it.'

Be frank when placing the dots. Do you really understand the technology? Do you really understand the market? And are you really well organized to offer this product in this market? Is your organization familiar with the business model you intend? There is no 'good' or 'bad' position in the model. Just a frank indication of how you feel about your effort today. Draw the matrix, mark the X's, and keep the paper in the back of this book for later use (or use your phone to photograph the matrix).

CHAPTER 4
Continuous Change

In the coming decades, data will drive
continuous change

U p until the last few years, disruptive technology was easily recognizable as a mechanical toolset, a software application or perhaps even an app. The technology used in these tools offered novel ways of solving a specific problem. In Christensen's famous disruptive innovation example of the disk drive market (Christensen, The Innovator's Dilemma, 1997), the fledgling disk drive producer MiniScribe started shipping drives that were smaller and held less storage capacity than existing drives and quickly captured the market. The smaller drives serviced the then infant laptop market, which in turn would mushroom and eventually disrupt the market for desktop computers and their larger disk drives. The physical technology and technological improvements led to different product offerings that disrupted the market.

Over the last few years, not the hardware but software and data have become the all-powerful raw material for disruption. Data, the stuff that was long regarded as the by-product of hardware. The stuff that could be copied, transferred, split, mixed, matched, searched, and calculated at virtually no cost, with simple tools and with commonly available knowledge and skills.

Along with the development of more digitized products, gadgets, and gizmos came the steady stream of data generated by such devices. Car engines started collecting sensor data to optimize performance and aid engineers in maintenance. Roads and traffic lights were fitted with sensors to optimize the flow of traffic and reduce waiting times. Offices were fitted with smart-card access systems, registering who accessed which part of an office, when, and with whom. Each of these systems was disconnected from the other, and their data was used primarily for optimizing the function of the parent technology.

Then came a wave of connectivity technologies: Bluetooth, ubiquitous WiFi, RFID, and ultimately the smartphone and 4 and 5G networks. Data *from* everywhere could easily be transmitted *to* anywhere. The availability of data sparked an unprecedented wave of creativity in business, ready to use data to improve products and business models. With increasing demand, sensors and connected devices rapidly got smaller and connectivity distances increased by the introduction of long-range, low power networks, such as LoRaWAN. The 'Internet of Things' (a term coined by Procter & Gamble employee Kevin Ashton as early as 1999) developments reached mass-market somewhere between 2012 and 2014 and continues to grow exponentially. Present-day, data is being generated by factory machines, aircraft, cars, thermostats, coffee machines, toys, door locks, clothes, and contact lenses. All connected through apps and standardized digital interfaces.

Data has become an overarching technology that enables a deluge of new functions and applications. In the early years of the 21st century, the term '2.0' was used to describe a situation where analog products and services were being transformed into software. Competitive battles no longer focused on technical specifications but on features and user experience. Michael Porter, renowned for his scientific work on industry competition, wrote an influential article in Harvard Business Review in 2014 in which he demonstrates how smart, connected products reshape entire industries as they become part of 'system of systems' in which the exchange of data between these products can create value in an infinite number of ways. In the words of Porter this raises "strategic choices related to how value is created and captured, how the prodigious amount of new (and sensitive) data they generate is utilized and managed, how relationships with traditional business partners such as channels are redefined, and what role companies should play as industry boundaries are expanded." (Porter, 2014)

The period ahead will be defined by the power that lies captured in the data within those connected systems. This development first referred to by authors Mayer-Schoenberger and Kenneth

Cukier as 'datafication' (Mayer-Schoenberger, 2013), will transform and disrupt every single industry from the outside and from within.

Three value drivers for data

The '2.0 era,' at the time, seemed to be happening primarily in the many books, articles, and blogposts that were being written about it. The revolution in the way business was conducted and in how products were offered was easy to find for those who were in the business, but anything but overwhelming to the general public.

Digitization was what naturally happened: a steady stream of neat new websites, services, gadgets, and gizmos. And here we are, ordering our electronics and clothes online, using cloud-services for our e-mail and file storage, and we legally stream music and binge entire seasons of our favorite series in one single night. We know exactly what hit us, we just never noticed the impact. Datafication has many similar characteristics. The buzz in the media for one. Terminology such as Big Data, Internet of Things, Artificial Intelligence (AI), and Quantified Self feeds the feeling that change is in the air, yet again.

But ask anyone about the tangible effects and you probably end up discussing the self-driving car within minutes. And while most of us have never actually been in a self-driving car, we all encounter Big Data, Internet of Things, AI, and the Quantified Self almost on a daily basis. So, even though data-driven innovation feels like a distant development in a Silicon Valley garage, it is happening all around you. And it will impact your organization if it isn't already doing so. The trick to this development is that there is not just one way to use this impact to your advantage.

Data-driven innovation offers tangible advantages for organizations in multiple ways. Without aiming to provide a scientific classification of applications for data, I find that there is an easy to use rule of thumb that distinguishes three specific value drivers for data. For many clients in my consulting practice, these value drivers have proven to be extremely helpful in identifying why and how datafication adds value in operational and strategic decision making.

The use cases do not merely depend on the way data is used by an organization. It also depends on how familiar this organization is with the required technology and the markets it is used to serve.

What is important to realize, when determining the value of data for an organization, is the vantage point taken when assessing its potential. This vantage point is always the organization, never the 'perceived general market.' 'Data Analytics' is never just complex, it is *complex for a particular organization*. For some organizations, any form of data analytics may be considered 'high-tech' or 'complex,' simply because they lack resources or experience. For other companies, that same analytics capability may be considered basic knowledge. For them, other challenges are deemed 'complex,' perhaps something like Blockchain. So, when assessing the value of data, we take into consideration the impact that data has on the value propositions of that company.

In much the same way, the impact of data on a given market differs greatly per organization. For some organizations, the use of data offers opportunities to grow in existing markets. However, when more data is added, new value may be created for adjacent or even entirely new markets. Some companies may be well equipped to service both B2B and B2C markets, but others will find value in data to service private individuals, only to discover that servicing consumers requires an organization completely different from the one needed to service corporate clients.

The impact of data on products and markets, when depicted in a single matrix, offers a model for the three value drivers. Throughout this book, I will expand this matrix into a model describing three plateaus of digital transformation.

The impact of data on products and markets

1. Analysis for performance optimization

The lowest hanging fruit in extracting value from data is the analysis of data to find areas for improvement in an *existing* organization. Banks, for instance, can analyze which customers are likely to overdraw on their accounts and proactively offer them a loan or a larger credit facility.

This field of analytics is not new at all. It has been around for years under familiar terms such as Business Intelligence, Consumer Analytics, and Corporate Performance Management. In the last ten years, the volume of data that has been created by companies has increased so much that new technologies have emerged to manage and analyze that data. Data Analytics has offered numerous new analytical strategies that can further optimize existing performance of organizations. It can even discover previously undeterminable areas of improvement, for instance through the rigorous analysis of detailed consumer behavior that was previously impossible to research.

2. New products and services

Rather than using data as a tool to analyze the 'going concern', data can be used to improve or expand existing product offerings. Banks, for instance, can use data from customer transactions to offer a 'friendly reminder' service. Dutch bank 'Knab' (the word 'Bank' spelled backward in Dutch phonetically becomes the word 'smart') offers smart alerts to account holders, such as an alert when the same amount is paid twice to the same recipient in a single month. Different from the analytics example before, the bank does not use its data to analyze which customers would likely be in the market for a new loan, but instead uses the data to prevent customers from maxing out their credit. Not only is this a more consumer-friendly approach, Knab has found out that customers are actually willing to pay more for this kind of data-driven service than the company would make on additional interest payments.

3. Innovative solutions and new business models

Data, which originates as raw material from your organizations' primary processes, may be used to generate innovative new services or even new business models. Payroll processor ADP found that the data in 60 million monthly salary payments offer clear predictions on economic developments and built an entire business analyzing and reporting on the data generated by its core activity. This business, ADP Research Institute, is estimated to generate in excess of US$100 million annually.

In a similar way, commodity providers increasingly find new value-adding services in data derived from the provisioning of their commodity products, such as electricity. By collecting data from the use of appliances in a household, utilities can offer specific products and services, such as home automation and security. Some utilities even go so far as to provide the electricity for free. (Spijker, 2014)

Beyond Ansoff

There is a potential pitfall in the interpretation of the value drivers above, as datafication may be regarded as yet another technology to make products and services smarter. The three value drivers could easily be interpreted as the different growth strategies in Ansoff's famous growth matrix. But the value of data lies not in product development alone. It goes beyond. The impact of digital technology on products and markets has become more sophisticated. While this book is by no means an attempt to undermine the value of Ansoff's work, the impact of datafication requires taking an additional dimension into account when devising a growth strategy.

To explain why and how, first let's take a closer look at the original matrix. The Ansoff matrix, developed in 1957 by Russian/American economist Igor Ansoff, stands as one of business' most prominent and widely used strategy models. The model describes four strategies to be considered, each depending on the combination of the novelty of a market or a product, judging from the company's perspective.

When pondering the strategic direction of existing products in existing markets, Ansoff advises a 'market penetration' strategy. New product introductions in existing markets require a 'product development' strategy, and so on. It is tempting to plot innovative data-driven services into the category of 'new products' and opt for a product development strategy.

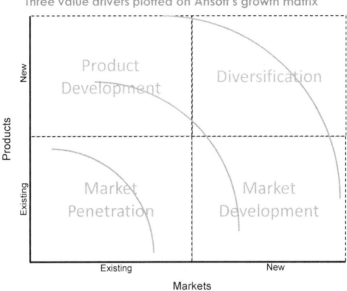

Three value drivers plotted on Ansoff's growth matrix

After all, if you were a car leasing company, data from onboard systems in cars could offer a new service to your client's fleet managers, who would be more than willing to pay extra for a reporting and analytics service detailing the travel history and maintenance requirements of each individual vehicle in the fleet. Such a service could potentially save your customers time and planning problems from unexpected maintenance, and your sales force would be eager to pitch the new value to existing clients.

In a different scenario, that same data from vehicles could enable 'pay-what-you-drive' services, which would allow your cars to be rented as a mobility service, in combination with air, train and taxi travel. This 'existing products in a new market' scenario is what Ansoff refers to as a 'market development' strategy. So far, the model holds true, even for data-driven products, services and even for business models. However, it holds true only when regarding 'the market' (or 'markets') as a constant. This is where data-driven innovations differ from traditional inventions and improvements.

Data-driven innovations, through the use of apps and web services, allow for immediate feedback and interaction with users. Often because of this interaction, such services are quickly regarded as the key feature or benefit of a product, even when layered on top of existing 'hardware' products. The digital components often are the closest, most visible part of the service. Think of the Uber app, being the product, even though a physical car takes you to your destination. Or the online learning environment which connects you with fellow students and tutors during a corporate training. The airline app, alerting you to a delayed flight or gate change. Ask any twenty-something and he or she will tell you that the banking app is the most prominent product their bank delivers to them.

The introduction of data-driven innovations is hardly ever an introduction of a new product into a particular market. Data-driven innovations tend to transform products by shifting focus from hardware to software. Because digital products and services have the ability to scale at tremendous speed, their impact is often disruptive to existing markets. Uber transformed the way we look at taxis and public transport, AirBnB disrupted parts of the travel market, and apps have changed the face of banking forever. This is why data-driven innovations take us beyond Ansoff's model: as they materialize, they change the very definitions of products and markets that the model defines.

Beyond an investment strategy

There is much content available in both scientific and popular management literature on the impact of innovation on corporate strategy. From this, a number of 'innovation strategy frameworks' have emerged that have gained traction and popularity in the business community. Their popularity comes from the fact that these frameworks provide a single verbatim and allow for transparent discussion on the topic. Although very relevant and useful to this day, the key focus of each of these frameworks is on managing investments in a portfolio of innovative options. I believe that current developments in digitization require a more extensive view of the topic that goes beyond investment management. First, I will briefly describe the most prominent frameworks:

- McKinsey's Three Horizons Framework
- McGrath's Opportunity Portfolio
- HBR's Adjacency Matrix

McKinsey's Three Horizons Framework

In 1999, McKinsey employees Mehrdad Baghai, Stephen Coley, and David White, published a book called *The Alchemy of Growth*. (Baghai, 1999) In it they presented what has become known as the 'Three Horizons Framework.' The framework depicts three investment horizons that leadership of organizations should focus on for sustainable growth of the organization.

Horizon One represents the core business of the current organization that provides the greatest profits and cash flow. Investments in innovation projects in this horizon are similar to the existing offerings, therefore create an almost immediate return on investment at relatively low risk.

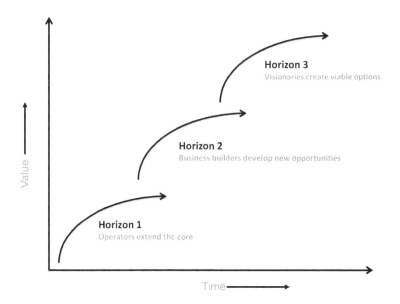

Horizon Two encompasses 'emerging opportunities,' often more distant from the current line of business, that require significant investments, bear substantial risk of failure, but that also are likely to generate substantial profits in the future.

Horizon Three, even further into the future, describes less tangible, potentially disruptive opportunities for growth further into the future at unknown risk with a high potential upside. The framework states that leadership should spend appropriate time on initiatives in each horizon and should find the right 'spread' of investments across the three horizons.

In 'The Entrepreneurial Mindset' (Gunther McGrath, 2000), Harvard scholar Rita Gunther McGrath and co-author Ian MacMillan describe innovation as a series of stages. Each stage is relative to the uncertainty of the technical or execution capability of the organization on the one hand, and the uncertainty of its market and organizational capabilities on the other.

McGrath's Opportunity Portfolio Matrix

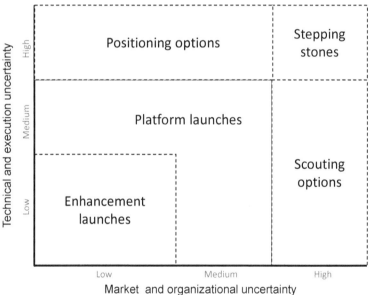

Innovations that are technically simple or easy to implement and can be executed in a known market and through existing organizational channels are called 'core enhancements.' These enhancements are relatively easy to achieve but also show a limited potential upside. In fact, most people would argue that these core enhancements are not innovations at all but just as their name suggests 'enhancements' of existing material.

Developments that are more complex – whether from a technical or market perspective – are dubbed 'platform launches.' These innovations are more challenging, and failure carries bigger risks, but they also offer bigger potential upsides. The kind of daring stuff that most people would describe as 'innovative' come with a high degree of technical and market uncertainty and are dubbed 'stepping stones' or 'options' towards the future.

From the perspective of corporate boardrooms, data-centric innovations are often regarded as 'stepping stones.' These innovations bypass known expertise and experience in the organization, often rely on complex and unknown technology, and address unknown and uncertain markets. Contrary to McKinsey's model, the authors do not emphasize the opportunity-side of each stage, but the relative uncertainty of each stage when viewed from the current position of the organization.

In 2012, Monitor Group's Bansi Nagji and Geoff Tuff published an article in Harvard Business Review (Nagji, 2012) that featured a model that has become known as the 'HBR Adjacency Matrix' (although the authors refer to it as the Innovation Ambition Matrix). Their matrix bears great resemblance to McKinsey's Three Horizons Matrix in the sense that it describes an investment strategy in three distances relative to the current business, but it more explicitly prescribes the target groups and product development strategies for each stage. Although not as broad in scope, in this area it more resembles McGrath's Matrix.

HBR's Adjacency Matrix

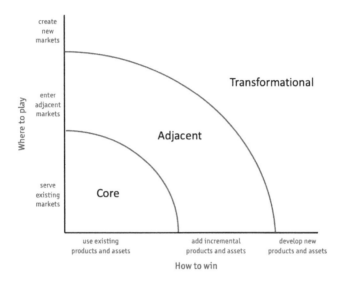

Again, Stage One describes core enhancements to the current organization's offerings. Stage Three describes disruptive or 'game-changing' innovations that require that "the company call on unfamiliar assets—for example, building capabilities to gain a deeper understanding of customers, to communicate about products that have no direct antecedents, and to develop markets that aren't yet mature." Between them is Stage Two, which is labeled the 'Adjacency' stage, where innovation involves leveraging something the company does well into a new space.

After presenting the stages, the authors go into more detail about how to balance investments across all stages, with the conclusion that most investments should go to Stage Three (on average 70%, versus 20% to Stage Two and 10% to Stage One), as these innovations will generate the biggest future return on investment.

A strategy for investment, speed, and change

The ideas presented in this book are in line with the ideas of McKinsey, McGrath, and HBR in the sense that innovation presents opportunities for growth at various stages in the future and at varying distances from the existing company. They also state that such opportunities should be carefully managed by senior leadership. This book adds to these ideas in two ways: The first way is that Continuous Innovation stresses the fact that digital technology greatly increases the speed of innovation. This creates a necessity for an investment strategy that facilitates the speed of development through the various stages from the top-right down, rather than separate investments in each separate stage.

The second is that both McKinsey's and Harvard's theories reason from the assumption that the current organization will remain the same across the development of innovations in each stage. It does not. Each innovation in 'Horizon Two/adjacency' and 'Horizon Three/transformation' drives changes in the organization's processes and design. This creates a new vantage point with each new innovation and requires leadership to not only manage investments, but also to continuously manage the flow of innovations from Horizon Three, to Horizon Two and into the current operation and to manage organizational change accordingly.

CHAPTER 5
The Corporate Catch-22

Innovation tends to undermine
existing business models

As technology advances and more data is generated, this data increasingly often becomes available to other players than those who generated it. Apps, sensors, and web services all work to collect data from as many sources as possible, making it difficult for organizations to stop third parties from using their data.

For incumbent businesses, uncertain times are yet again ahead. Since the sudden rise of high-tech Internet startups at the turn of the century, corporations have been under attack from high-tech, infant businesses. And yet again, even the best-organized corporations appear to have no clear answer to the disruptive power of teenagers in t-shirts. And while the long-revered stability and trustworthiness of the financial sector took a nosedive in public opinion, startup founders and entrepreneurs have risen to rock star status to fill the void. They are Schumpeter's entrepreneurs, causing gales of creative destruction.

As a result, Amazon's and NY Times' bestseller lists in management literature have been overflowing with startup success stories, "how-to" videos, self-help guides to entrepreneurship and lessons in startup methods and principles. All attention goes out to 'Exponential Organizations', 'Lean Startup', and 'Digital Disruption'. And none of these books sells the idea that well organized, well researched, and carefully planned execution of technological advances is the way forward. Instead, they sell the notion that the startup is the only successful form of organization and that data is its raw material – as though digital disruption was the only way forward and corporate organizations were, by nature, incapable of innovation or disruption.

However, developments in technology and business have led to a situation where the current organizational and business models for large organizations have become out of sync with their environment. Production of goods and products in most cases requires assets and infrastructure that are complex to operate and capital intensive to own. Yet the marketable value of these goods is increasingly driven by data. This data is no longer the exclusive property of the organization that created it through its assets. It is quickly becoming easily available to third parties, through for instance apps and online connections, allowing third parties to harvest the data-driven value without owning the assets. This leaves manufacturers with complex, capital intensive production facilities competing with low cost, high margin technology companies over their most lucrative data-driven services.

The paradox of asset-centric business models

This 'data vs. assets-dilemma' presents corporate organizations with a classic "Catch-22" situation. In a digitizing world, the business model for asset-centric production is increasingly reliant on services that are based on the data that originates from use of the product. However, both technological developments and customer demand exert pressure to allow free availability of this data to third parties, thereby undermining the very business model that supports the manufacturing of the product and its data.

A good example of such a Catch-22 situation can be found in the automotive industry. There's a good chance that it has escaped your attention, but for the last few years, an outright war on control over data from cars has been raging. Cars produce regular streams of data, such as measurements about the performance of the engine and key systems, fuel consumption, and oil pressure. Alongside this data comes data from all sorts of sensors and mobile devices including drive and driver behavior (braking, acceleration, staying in your lane), distance to other cars (adaptive cruise control), location (GPS), and who drives when (derived from seat presets). This data is available to almost anyone using what is called an 'On Board Diagnostics' device, or OBD. This device is easily installed by drivers into a slot in the dashboard that is also used by maintenance teams to download performance data to service-computers.

Third-party developers already offer apps that allow car owners to download this data and assess any performance issues. What used to be a brand-prerogative to attract car owners to brand-specific service centers is no longer a competitive advantage. Any service center can download the data and service the vehicle.

Car maintenance is not likely to be the only incentive for extracting car data. US-based startup Metromile uses car data to offer 'pay-per-mile' insurance. Canadian solutions provider GoFleet offers full fleet management solutions based on OBD data, and European ULU offers remote monitoring services for leasing, fleet management, and car repair. These initiatives take potential service and market share away from existing players in the field like Ford, BMW, and Toyota.

One step beyond conventional business models in the car industry, data sharing allows new types of insurance, corporate fleet management, and green-driving initiatives, bypassing existing markets and incumbent players. Already in 2011, Machina Research, a Gartner-owned research company specialized in research on connected devices, forecasted that by 2022 there will be over 700 million connected cars providing data to a US $1.1 billion aftermarket in devices for services.

Texas-based startup Vinli capitalizes on this development by offering a cloud platform to connect drivers and application developers. Through Vinli, any car owner can connect his or her car to enable the exchange of data with apps from developers that are also connected to the platform. In effect, Vinli aims to become the default platform for car-data exchange, bypassing car manufacturing brands as well as existing in-car entertainment and navigation providers such as TomTom. In late 2015, Vinli received a US $ 6.5 million investment from, of all possible candidates, Samsung.

Is it bad for companies like General Motors, Honda, and Mercedes to miss out on this kind of opportunity? Schumpeter would state that it is the inevitable start of a new business cycle. Christensen will argue that the incumbents should have been on the lookout for disruptive innovations. Yet it may just be that the developments in the car-data landscape are so many, so diverse, and so rapidly evolving that it is near impossible for each individual company to assess the direction and pace of developments to effectively claim a stake in the new market.

Connected car expert and entrepreneur Liz Slocum Jensen created an overview of the connected-car market and identified over 250 companies working on 56 topics on the subject (Slocum Jensen, 2016). This number, although not verified or in any way scientific, is roughly twice the number mentioned in similar estimates a year before. Research and consulting giant PWC Strategy& estimates the future to be bright for anyone but the incumbent players. In its 'Connected Car Report 2016', the company states that "70 percent of global connected service sales come from premium brands. By 2022, that number will fall to 50 percent, at the expense of falling margins." Later the report mentions that "…The balance of $120 billion may be captured by new entrants, including suppliers of new technology, mobility services, or digital services. Many of today's manufacturers and suppliers lack the skill, agility, and boldness to turn their companies digital quickly enough to take advantage of this change" (Viereckl, 2016).

Although today's manufacturers will not be able to take advantage of this change, it is too simple to attribute this fact to a lack of skill or agility. In fact, both skill and agility can be developed by the incumbents in a reasonable time. Over the last decade, lean working methods such as Lean Six Sigma and Agile working have risen in popularity and have been adopted by many incumbent firms. One of the leading 'modern' management principles, Lean, even originated at car manufacturer Toyota. And traditionally corporations have been very good at bringing their volume and wealth to bear to quickly solve problems and conquer markets. So why not now? Several factors are relevant:

1. Incumbents protect their past investments

2. Incumbents use agility to improve efficiency instead of adaptability

3. Incumbents assimilate acquisitions rather than adapt to them

4. Incumbents undervalue digital, data-driven markets

Incumbents protect past investments

Incumbent organizations represent a significant value for their shareholders. They protect their past capital investment by rewarding risk-averse behavior. This strategy makes sense because the potential rewards for risky behavior in large companies are small. After all, unlike startups, incumbents are not likely to multiply in size tenfold or more. Their markets are quite stable and sizeable. Their operating models require expensive assets and thousands of employees and consequently, incumbents do not scale very well.

Established companies are usually organized around achieving relatively low-profit margins in predictable, large markets. Because of the low margins, tuning efficiency is lucrative, and change is the natural enemy of efficiency. Adapting to change is, consequently, counterproductive to the company's goals. Yet technological advances and datafication have created an environment where change is not only inevitable but also increasing in speed. In this environment, incumbents find themselves caught between a rock and a hard place. Relying on what they do best, most incumbents focus on incremental improvements of existing offerings and implementation of technology to further improve efficiency.

Incumbents improve efficiency, not adaptability

In the last five years, Lean and Agile working methods have become quite popular in many organizations. The 'Lean' principles were originally developed by Toyota in the 1980s and are aimed primarily at increasing efficiency and reduction of waste, both in material and in time.

Agile working was invented in the early 2000s in the software industry with the aim to better address customer needs by reducing the development time of new applications. Both methods are today being used to increase effectiveness and flexibility of teams. In a nutshell, Lean and Agile principles aim to achieve more value for customers by working in short, nimble iterations rather than large planned projects and by adapting to change rather than planning towards a predefined goal based on assumptions.

Although many positive results have been achieved using Lean and Agile principles in the lower echelons of organizations, many large companies struggle to implement them at a larger scale. The reason for this is primarily that governance and control mechanisms are geared towards risk-mitigation. Agile projects with no predefined and planned outcome prove to be difficult to manage within the boundaries of corporate reporting structures. As a result, Lean and Agile methods are most often used by corporations to obtain higher output and less waste, rather than to increase the flexibility and adaptability of the organization.

By contrast, startups use Lean and Agile working to create a hyper-adaptive organization that will continuously tune itself to delivering the most value to its customers. An increasing number of scale-ups (startups that have become quite large themselves) such as LinkedIn, Spotify, and Uber have been able to retain their flexibility, even at scale.

Incumbents assimilate acquisitions, they do not adapt to them

In a bid to adopt new market innovations, many incumbents acquire startups that invented technological breakthroughs or created innovative business models. A popular mantra in corporate acquisition of innovative technology is to 'acquire early,' pointing to the success factor of acquiring promising startups in their very early stages of growth.

This poses somewhat of a problem to most incumbent managers after the acquisition. On the one hand, they need to intervene as little as possible in the startup's growth path. The startup should be protected from speed-limiting corporate regulations and cadence, preferably outside of corporate headquarters. On the other hand, they want to assimilate the new technology in the corporate business as quickly as possible to leverage the corporate scale and market power. Integrating innovative technology into an existing process is difficult enough as it is, so physical and cultural distance between the startup and the incumbent should be as small as possible.

But when the acquired technology turns out to be disruptive to the existing offering, the corporate tenure will resist change and force the new product into existing processes. After all, corporate culture is typically geared towards efficiency and not change. The result is often that the newly acquired technology is not nearly as effective as expected or hoped.

Incumbents undervalue digital, data-driven markets

Innovation is difficult. Not only because it requires a certain degree of future prediction but also because it requires people to view their existing markets in a different way. Incumbents have every incentive to maximize profits in existing markets. The entire organization is geared towards these markets and their operating models. Rethinking market dynamics based on innovative technology that resembles the current market offerings is difficult enough. But when an intangible development such as datafication enters the equation, future prediction becomes close to fortune-telling. And market size becomes a dominant factor.

Consider the following example. For a group of executives at Ford, it will be very feasible to assess the impact of the self-driving car in the market. The self-driving car is close to the existing concept of producing and selling cars. It is very realistic that Ford may develop such a car itself, even though it may not harbor the technological skills at this time. And most executives will be able to address the effect of self-driving cars on the ownership of cars in professional and consumer markets. Although it is realistic to assume that the total market for cars may drop significantly, Ford may still be a dominant player in the future market.

Now consider the market for data-driven products and services using in-car data, and their effect on the car market. PWC predicts that the market for these services will be in the order of US$150 billion by 2022. The company calculated that in order to achieve this revenue, car manufacturers will need to sell six times more connected car service packages than they will be capable of. With data being easily exportable from the car to external devices, the potential for third party vendors for selling connected services is over 80% of the market, being US$120 billion. Now that may sound like a big red flag for the automotive market. But it isn't. The current market volume in cars is around US$1,500 billion, ten times the size of the estimated connected car services market by 2022. If each manufacturer would obtain a market share in the connected services market relative to its current market share, Ford would have a turnover of less than 0.5% of its total revenue stream, assuming the connected services market follows the annual growth rate of 25% predicted by PWC. With profitability being half of its major rivals and in the midst of explosive growth of car sales in BRIC (Brazil, Russia, India, and China) and a very threatening position of the Chinese carmaking industry, Ford executives will likely opt to sit back and see what happens.

What is interesting in this decision is not so much the monetary reasoning, but the reasoning from the premise that the car market will remain the same until 2022 and in the years to follow. It does not consider the fact that between now and the next few years 80% of the market initiative will lie in the hands of third-party vendors who have no incentive whatsoever to benefit the car manufacturers.

Vendors will seek to leverage new business models and opportunities for car-sharing, self-driving cars, hybrid mobility solutions, and other means to disrupt the existing market for car manufacturing. They will build networks with infrastructure operators, financiers and insurers, providers of parking and charging services and other third parties, leveraging the full extent of the connected car.

The innovative data market is not likely to have an immediate impact in the existing markets and product categories of incumbents. This makes sense and follows every theory in innovation known today, including Schumpeter's business cycles and Christensen's disruptive innovation theory. But unlike Schumpeter's and Christensen's theories, data-driven innovations will not just replace an existing offering by a seemingly inferior one, they will change the dynamics of the market altogether and at a pace far greater than has previously been seen. And herein lies the danger for the existing finance-centric method of evaluation of the potential of data-driven innovation. Data-driven innovations often provide but a fraction of the turnover and revenue of traditional products and services.

For that reason, senior management frequently disregards the potential of the innovations as 'not relevant,' and either defer the initiative to middle management or disband the idea altogether. This is just one example of the typical way in which disruptive innovations get dismissed as 'inferior products for insignificant markets.' These disruptors, however, drive a market that requires fewer and often cheaper assets, that scales exponentially faster, and that is continuously open to new entrants. By financially comparing data-driven initiatives to the financial scope of the existing markets, incumbents tend to lose the battle before it has even begun.

All dressed up and nowhere to go

When reading the above, one might wonder if corporates stand any chance at all of producing successful innovations. They are slow and resistant to change. Not seldom will popular management literature underline these weaknesses, providing a coup-de-grace by bringing up start-up culture. Ask any startup employee about why he/she works for a startup rather than in a corporation and you'll get roughly the same answer: startup culture is in a category of its own. Incredible team spirit, inventing the next big thing, proximity to customers, absence of hierarchy and protocol, and the possibility of becoming an IPO-millionaire. In fact, the startup culture often is directly linked to the outright rejection of corporate culture. No suits, no managerial hierarchy, no elaborate and slow processes! Long live innovation!

But corporate culture has a few advantages that startups simply cannot offer their hard-working devotees that actually makes them potentially far more successful at innovation than startups; we will examine some of them in the following sections.

Corporations own and control large markets

Incumbent businesses own and control sizeable markets. They offer products and services to an existing customer base – customers who know and trust their company and are easy to approach. Customers who are often willing to provide feedback on new offerings and ideas. And who provide continuous streams of data about their needs and use of the products and services. A tremendously valuable and easily approachable platform to test new ideas, get real market feedback and scale quickly. Startups need to spend most of their effort on creating a solid market and user base, corporates have it right at their fingertips.

Corporations leverage well-trained workforces

Incumbents often have sizeable and skilled workforces. More importantly, incumbents have the resources and scale to train for excellence and exchange their experience and best practices from the market. In addition, incumbents often operate highly skilled HR departments that are able to attract top talent from university as well as seasoned veterans. They may not seem to be attractive employers from a 'startup-culture' perspective, but when push comes to shove, incumbents can leverage a well-trained workforce extremely quickly to build, market and deliver innovative solutions.

Corporations have deep pockets

Especially compared to startup businesses, incumbent businesses can have access to considerable financial resources. Corporate agencies certainly will not throw large sums of money at just anything, but when they do decide to invest in innovative projects, they usually do so in a scale beyond the possibilities of startups.

Corporations own steady streams of data

Incumbents have the ability to generate data from the use of existing products and services by existing customers. This data allows them to assess usage of the existing offerings, create improved products and services and offers a unique starting point for data-driven innovations. Data is the source of digital disruption.

So why, if they own the sources, are incumbents not capable of defending themselves against disruptive technologies? Well, the simple answer provided by Christensen is that incumbents do not feel as if they are under attack. Startups are not out to get incumbents. They aim to win a market for themselves, regardless of who they are taking it from. Corporates hardly notice the lost market share at first, because startups initially only tend to win over 'early adopters' and not the vast majority of customers. Profit margins and market shares of incumbents deteriorate only at a barely detectable pace.

For the corporation to be disrupted, management will argue, the disruptive innovation must offer a solution to a problem with the same 'modus operandi.' When Christensen describes the example of disruptive mini-mills in steel manufacturing in his book 'The Innovators Dilemma,' he describes how mini-mills are disruptive to large steel mills, but they are steel mills nonetheless. And that is where data-driven innovations often differ. Disruptive innovations in data-driven strategy often provide a whole new approach to a solution. In the steel example, they are comparable to replacing the need for steel altogether. Data-driven disruptive innovations do not disrupt the market for steel mills, they disrupt the market for steel.

Even though incumbents often own a mountain of disruptive raw material, it would work against them to use it. This is the crux of the "Catch-22" for corporations: the current primary process creates data that allows disruption of that very process. Using the data in a major effort to disrupt oneself is a hard sell to shareholders. Not using it, in this digital day and age, would mean missing out on many incremental improvements that set it back against its competitors. That too is a hard sell to impatient shareholders. So, most incumbents opt for incremental innovation: they release more digital applications with, and as part of, their products and services, generating data that becomes available to customers and third parties. Once available in the market, the data becomes raw material for new digital innovations.

In the early stages, these digital innovations will not replace the incumbent market in one big bang. Yet the technology scales so easily that, once it catches on, the pace of disruption is often felt as a revolution in much the same way as Christensen's original 'disruptive innovation' mechanism. Because digital technology is relatively easy to acquire and master, almost everyone is capable of data-driven disruption. Furthermore, ideas and inspiration are easily shared and spread. Investment capital is relatively easy to obtain, and global distribution of services comes at virtually no extra cost. In a global digital marketplace, disruption is becoming the norm, rather than the revolution and offers a constant threat to incumbents. Not the threat of having their market share taken away from them by new entrants, but the threat of having new markets created around them continuously.

"It's life, Jim, but not as we know it"

Digital disruption adheres to Christensen's original principles of disruptive innovation: new entrants begin by successfully targeting previously undervalued segments with a different solution to the problem. They gain a foothold by delivering more suitable functionality in a non-comparable solution type. Incumbents, not recognizing the new solution as a threat to its most profitable customer segments, tend not to respond vigorously. Entrants then move upmarket, improving and expanding the performance that incumbents' mainstream customers require. When these customers adopt the entrants' offerings in volume, disruption has occurred. Digital disruption is different to the original definition in the sense that:

a) The disruptive solution is not specifically cheaper or inferior in functionality than the disrupted solution, but it offers a different approach to the original problem and solution.

b) The disruptive solution does not necessarily target a non- or low-profitable segment, but a segment specifically prone to the new type of solution, often not even regarded as a specific segment of users in the 'old' market.

Digital disruption is so difficult to tackle for incumbents because it does not follow the rules of the existing game. Incumbents have built risk-mitigating organizations around a product-market fit with only a certain degree of flexibility to innovate products. They have tremendous difficulties when they are required to quickly adapt to radically changing markets and new business models.

Digital products tend to completely overhaul the value proposition of the goods sold. The innovation manager of a large Finnish publisher once told me that their brand-new mobile news app was "not a news app, but an instrument for our customers to fight boredom." That notion changed their view on the value of news and consequently on the business model for the app. Within months, the app, which published news and infotainment as bite-sized short articles and videos for easy and fast consumption when waiting for a train or riding an elevator, gained an overwhelming market share, pushing traditional news providers out of the market altogether.

Similarly, markets are no longer defined by traditional characteristics such as region, customer demographics, or distribution strategies. Digital technology and datafication allow markets to become dynamic, with consumers continuously belonging to one or more customer segments based on variables such as personal preferences, behavior, location, and purchase history.

The same technology allows organizations to create adaptive products that automatically adjust their features and benefits depending on the customer it then serves. No two Spotify customers listen to the same personalized radio station. And customers do not regard Amazon as a bookstore (or any store for that matter), but as a recommendation engine with seamless purchasing options. It's like comparing apples and pears. Even when Amazon opened a physical bookstore in Seattle in 2016, it did not adhere to traditional definitions of the market for books retail. Even from the perspective of Pam Cady, manager at Seattle's 116-year-old University Book Store and now under immediate threat from Amazon, Amazon's physical store is a completely alien operation: "[it is] a bookstore for people who don't care about being in a real bookstore", she tells Julia Carry Wong, a reporter from The Guardian in an interview in 2016 (Wong, 2016). Perhaps the behavior of digitally disrupted markets is best described by a famous quote from Mr. Spock from the popular Star Trek series when he describes a seemingly inexplicable phenomenon in outer space to Captain James T. Kirk: "It's life, Jim, but not as we know it..."

Netflix and Spotify are well-known examples that illustrate how many digital disruptions do not necessarily follow the tracks of Christensen's disruptive innovation, even though they harbor the same effect. Netflix, the online (streaming) video service, is often mentioned as the disruptor of the video rental industry, and the Blockbuster retail stores in particular. But by Christensen's definition, Netflix was not a disruptive innovation – it did not target a low-end part of the market and it offered a service that could equal or even outperform Blockbuster in features or quality. Even when it did not yet stream content over the internet, but sent DVDs through the regular mail, Netflix boasted a greater selection and a subscription payment model, rather than pay-per-movie with annoying late-return fees.

Even though Netflix customers could not watch their movie the same day, they did not regard that as 'low-end' or 'less quality.' Instead, customers saw the advantage over having to physically go out to the store not knowing if the DVD was even available. In addition, Netflix users could keep the DVD for as long as they required and never paid late fees. With Blockbuster relying heavily on late fees as a major part of their income model, Netflix was disruptive because it offered better service by redefining the market. It wasn't so much the service quality or particular target group, it was the business model that ultimately put Netflix on top of Blockbuster (Satell, 2014).

PART II
Three Plateaus of
Innovation Strategy

CHAPTER 6
Innovation Strategy Matrix

Rapid Evolution always
beats Revolution

D ata, disruption, and innovation have become entangled terminology. Somehow with the rise of the economies in the United States and Europe after the financial crisis, a new tech startup-bubble emerged that, at least in popular press, suggested that startups equal innovation and that innovation equals disruption. Backed by real market examples such as Uber, AirBnB, and Google's self-driving car, the startup was hailed as the chariot of fire in the arena of business.

Although corporations, to this day, are often seen as valuable sources of data, they are deemed too slow to innovate. They are often urged to 'disrupt themselves before the market does it.' Unfortunately, there is substantial empirical evidence to support the notion that this strategy is, in many cases, not just disruptive but also destructive. Inspired, or at least seemingly threatened, by technological advancements around them, many corporations try to leapfrog into new markets with innovative, data-driven products, using the latest in startup principles and work methods. Even though they are backed by corporate 'funds and firepower,' many corporate innovation initiatives never reach their targets. Rarely is this due to a lack of potential, but more often because their initiators failed to consider that digital innovation changes not just the rules of the game but the game itself. Even though they adjust their products and services and even some of their methods and tools, incumbents usually fail to adapt their organization and processes to their new environment and, consequently, become disrupted anyway.

Data-driven innovation is subject to what I like to call 'the gravitational pull' of technological and organizational change. Whenever organizations introduce more data-driven technology in their products and services, they will need to adapt to servicing clients and markets in a different way. Data-driven technology requires different organization structures and processes. Hence, when data-driven projects yield results, they will, without exception, impact existing processes and drive organizational change. For those organizations that set out to use data to achieve optimization in the existing processes and organization, success may quickly disguise itself as unwanted side effects and render the project a failure.

In the next few chapters, I will further explain why this is the case and how corporations can break free from datafication's 'self-fulfilling failure.'

Revolution: Rapid evolution

In Chapter One of his book *Bold* (Diamandis, Bold: How to Go Big, Create Wealth and Impact the World, 2015), Peter Diamandis presents the case of Kodak and how the company missed out on the opportunity to take a leading role in digital photography. He refers to Kodak as being ignorant for not seeing the opportunities of digital photography in the 1970s when one of its own employees invented the 0.1-megapixel camera. Diamandis criticizes Kodak management for remaining strategically stuck to paper and film, the core business, and not noticing the exponential powers of digital cameras, a technology that could render much of Kodak's asset base obsolete.

But in the 1970s, the Internet was practically non-existent and the connotation of the word 'digital' was a far cry from what it means today. Seeing the full potential of digital cameras at that time required making incredible assumptions about future technology developments, even to the point where such assumptions bordered on plain fortune-telling. Although it is undeniable that Kodak management made serious errors in judging the potential of digital photography in the '70s and '80s, not taking an all-out bet on the digital camera in the 1970s was not one of them.

Modern corporate agencies seem to face the same situation in digital transformation and datafication scenarios: the heavyweight of existing business simply makes huge 'stepping-stone' innovation strategically impractical. Why invest in something with extremely high risk and uncertain potential? Many tech startups go all-in and spend a fortune in venture capital on a promise that, more often than not, doesn't materialize.

What would make it that an incumbent, with precious resources tied to running an already competitive business, spend its precious working capital on such an uncertainty? Incumbents use capital to create an efficient organization optimized for the current competitive battles. Why jeopardize existing competitive positions with investments in massive uncertainty?

The answer is because it is not the wise thing to do. Data-driven innovation does not rely on stepping-stone innovations and great fortune for success. It does not take an all-important bet on the development of technology. Instead, it takes sound reasoning about the speed of change that envelops the market. Harnessing that change does not call for revolution, but for rapid evolution: a structured process of high paced, manageable, iterative change. It calls for improving existing business through core enhancements while step-by-step building the platform launches of the future. And in the meantime, experimentation with some (perhaps seemingly crazy) 'stepping stones' to determine the general direction of future growth. Underlying all this development and experimentation is the need for a clear understanding of what data really is and which potential changes it unlocks in markets, customers, and organizations.

It is easy to confuse innovation with high-tech startups, but in fact, most tech startups do not create disruptive technologies and many disruptive technologies do not originate in startups. Google and Apple, widely regarded as two of the most innovative companies in the world, took decades to reach their current position and killed many, if not most, of their innovative darlings in all stages of development.

These two companies have mastered the art of rapidly nursing innovations to fruition. Although they do not shy away from attempting dazzlingly crazy challenges, the leaders of both companies despise a senseless, high-risk approach. Nowhere is the path of innovation better described than in the letter that Google founder Larry Page penned for the launch of Alphabet (Google's new parent company) on September 1st, 2015:

> "As Sergey and I wrote in the original founders' letter 11 years ago, "Google is not a conventional company. We do not intend to become one." As part of that, we also said that you could expect us to make "smaller bets in areas that might seem very speculative or even strange when compared to our current businesses." From the start, we've always strived to do more, and to do important and meaningful things with the resources we have.
>
> We did a lot of things that seemed crazy at the time. Many of those crazy things now have over a billion users, like Google Maps, YouTube, Chrome, and Android. And we haven't stopped there. We are still trying to do things other people think are crazy but we are super excited about.
>
> We've long believed that over time companies tend to get comfortable doing the same thing, just making incremental changes. But in the technology industry, where revolutionary ideas drive the next big growth areas, you need to be a bit uncomfortable to stay relevant."

This investor's letter highlights clearly the attention that Page and Brin paid to the top-right corner of the Opportunity Portfolio: Stepping Stones. They did "things that seemed crazy at the time." These things indeed, as Page states, now have become normal and business as usual, boasting over a billion users as proof. Google Maps, when first initiated by Google, was nothing short of a weird idea. Google Books doubled down by stirring fierce debate about Google's attack on copyrights and awe about the sheer scale of the intention to digitize all books in the world.

Over the course of 10 years, we have grown accustomed to some of these impressive innovations. And yes, some of them actually have over a billion users. But many more died along the way. Not many people remember Google Health, a place where people could upload their medical records and allow Google to provide them with information on conditions and potential allergies. Or Google Lively, Google's alternative to the virtual reality world, Second Life. Even the high-profile, much revered Google Glass eventually was scrapped.

Google's strategy shows that 'innovation' is not placing a big bet on the single 'next big thing.' And even though innovation 'happens at the fringes' and some of the company's ideas seem crazy, innovation is serious business. Innovation is the single force driving Google's success and each previously 'radical' innovation drives the next wave. Today, some people may laugh about Google's failures, but Google does not regard them as such. For Google, the failures are attempts at creating new markets. Most fail, but some achieve astounding success. Those who laugh at Google's mistakes are also more than likely to use some of the attempts that paid off. Such as the free online search in any of the millions of books that Google has manually scanned, which seemed crazy at the time. Or the ability to take a peek in almost any street (and lately also in public buildings and stores) in the world using Street View, which seemed not just crazy, but outright impossible both in execution and in business model. In the same way, many people currently talk about a few more things that Google is now undertaking that 'seem crazy in this time.' Google's Loon project, for instance, aiming to launch a network of balloons over Africa to provide the continent with free wireless internet. Or Project Wing, where the company develops a delivery service using autonomous drones. Yet is likely that we will be using some of these ideas in the near future. In any case, not many people doubt that in a few years' time, many of us will actually be using cars that are using Google's self-driving technology. Google's relentless focus on innovation through 'crazy' ideas have made it one of the largest and most influential organizations in the world. So how crazy then is Calico, Google's not very well known but nothing-short-of-substantial effort to combat life's most daunting problem: mortality itself?

Obviously, not all organizations have Google's cultural DNA to reach for ever 'crazier' ideas. But what all organization can and should learn from Google's success is that there is no such thing as 'revolutionary innovation'. Even Google grows from one idea to the next, in the full awareness that many attempts at innovation will fail along the way. There is no room for complacency. The way forward is to continuously evolve from one idea to the next.

Three plateaus of innovation strategy

Information Technology itself has developed along the lines of the stages suggested by McKinsey, HBR, and McGrath. Technology first allowed organizations to optimize their existing operations by automating tasks, becoming more efficient or faster. Simplified: they kept doing what they had always been doing, but better, using more technology. When computers were introduced to businesses in the 1960s and '70s, publishers quickly recognized their potential to replace their existing linotype machines that were used for typesetting the newspaper for the printing press. They used computer technology to speed up the process of printing, initially through a technology called 'computer-to-film' and later by 'computer-to-plate'. Time savings not only meant a reduction in production costs, but also that deadlines could be extended, so the newspaper could report on news from a later time the previous day.

The advent of even more complex technology, the internet, meant that improvements for businesses could not only save time or money, but could introduce entirely new features and functionalities. The internet allowed organizations to create an easy to use interface between their customers and their technology. This further increased efficiency and speed, but more importantly, allowed for entirely new digitized processes in the delivery of products and services to clients. The publisher in the previous example now had the means to publish content not just once a day, but 24/7. This impacted the publisher's core processes, changed its product offerings, and effectively demanded a new type of organization to run the company.

Today, in the age of datafication, a new plateau is opening up. Technology has come to the point where data can be easily separated from its origin and copied, shared, and used with almost anyone or anything. This allows for the creation of new and improved products and services and ultimately for the development of innovative and even disruptive business models.

Remember our publisher? Over the last few years, the organization has found it tremendously difficult to get consumers to purchase a subscription to its online publications. After all, publishers nowadays compete with the likes of Twitter and Facebook, which regularly provide free and fast entertainment and news. The publishers have a distinct advantage, though: they can use their structured content to profile consumer behavior across their websites, collecting vast amounts of data about consumers' interests and needs. Such insights could be turned into highly personalized subscriptions that consumers *are* willing to pay for. Or they could be used for highly targeted advertising at a premium price. Or, even more valuable, the insights can be repackaged and sold as behavioral insights to third parties such as retailers, manufacturers, and even local governments. The old business model can give way to an entirely new proposition. This type of innovative business model usage is described in more detail in my book 'The New Oil: Using Innovative Business Models to Turn Data Into Profit.' (Spijker, 2014)

When plotting data-driven innovation on McKinsey's Three Horizons Framework, McGrath's Opportunity Portfolio Matrix or HBR's Adjacency Matrix, it becomes obvious that the innovations flow from the top right (Horizon Three) to the bottom left (Horizon One). What were once 'crazy ideas' become 'business-as-usual' at an increasing rate.

It is important to realize, however, that it will not suffice to plot only the particular horizon in which an innovation is contained. Each innovation in itself, when adopted, changes the organizations business models and processes and therefore the organizational structure itself. With an increasing speed of innovations flowing from 'stepping stones' or Horizon Three downwards, the time allowed to adapt the organization to make optimal use of the innovation's potential shortens. Innovation and organizational change are merging, and a new capability is required to manage this development. It is no longer enough to monitor the flow of innovations down the horizons and respond to it. Instead, a strategy is needed to allow the organization to grow upwards and meet the innovation half-way.

The Innovation Strategy Matrix describes the dynamics of this process and separates it into three consecutive stages in which organizations take specific actions. Each stage, or plateau, acting as an invisible force, pushing the organization to the next level. I've named these plateaus Optimization, Transformation, and Innovation. In popular terms: Do what you always did using more data, develop new processes in existing business, and create new business models.

The Innovation Strategy Matrix

Plateau 1: *Optimize*

In the first plateau, organizations regard data-driven technology as a means to improve operational performance or reduce costs. Usually, the focus is placed on analyzing data to find room for improvement. With the vast improvement of analytical capabilities, especially over large and unstructured datasets commonly referred to as 'Big Data', new possibilities have come within reach that have made these improvements an attractive investment, often resulting in significant performance enhancement. More advanced applications of data in this stage can be found in automated decision making that relies on data analytics and systems that automatically act when certain thresholds are met.

Plateau 2: Transform

The second plateau is often the natural result of the first stage: when optimization of the existing process is well-executed, most organizations will automatically recognize the potential to take things one step further. With available analyses of processes and the automation of decision making and task execution, existing processes will quickly seem to become slow, cumbersome, and even downright foolish. The organization will find ways to adapt processes and ultimately products and propositions to the newly discovered possibilities. Although the organization will remain active in the same type of business, in many cases the way in which it conducts its operations changes. The 'platform' on which an organization operates changes altogether.

Plateau 3: Innovate

The third plateau is typically entered when the organization breaks the boundaries of traditional markets. It either creates new value propositions with business models that are disruptive to the status quo or starts to market data generated by its traditional core processes as a separate product or proposition. Even though in early stages the revenue from this type of proposition may be small and only supportive to the existing product portfolio, data-driven products and services have the potential to allow new business models and become key revenue generators. In doing so, such innovations often render the products and services that actually generate the data subordinate to the new value propositions. As I explained in 'The New Oil,' more and more companies achieve this 'flipping point' in data-driven business models.

Datafication's gravitational pull

Digital technology has grown from a constructed means to automate existing processes to an omnipresent force that continuously and relentlessly influences how we live our lives and conduct business. The application of technology is no longer a contemplated business choice, it has turned into a competitive race to discover new value and to apply it in the smartest way to deliver it to customers. The generic nature of digital technology and the worldwide development of new technology and its applications means that digital innovation has become a constant factor.

Few people have put it much clearer (or with a more refined sense of understatement) than my respected colleague, Mathias Cobben, when he stated in 2017 that "It is highly unlikely that in the future companies will analyze less data than they do today." Although his statement refers to data rather than to technology as a whole, it is not difficult to accept that it rings true for either one of them.

When you take a closer look at the two axes in the plateau model, they reveal an interesting and quite recognizable dynamic: each of the axes exerts a gravitational pull on the other axis. Whenever an organization applies more complex technology solely for the purpose of optimizing existing markets (moving 'up' from the bottom left of the matrix), it is essentially creating a complex and expensive infrastructure to optimize efficiency.

Ultimately, the capabilities offered by more complex technology will drive initiatives to apply the technology in innovative processes to address the needs of different markets in an attempt to gain a competitive advantage. The availability of the technology pushes development to the right of the matrix as if it was pulled back by the horizontal axis.

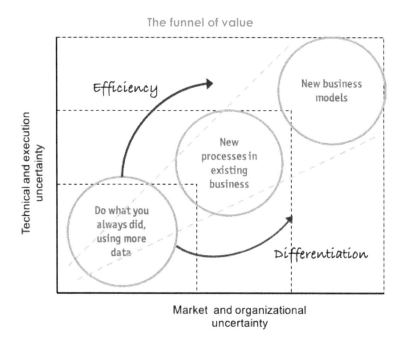

The funnel of value

New business models

Efficiency

New processes in existing business

Technical and execution uncertainty

Do what you always did, using more data

Differentiation

Market and organizational uncertainty

In much the same way, differentiation into new markets, or a purely horizontal move from the bottom left to the bottom right of the matrix, almost always opens opportunity for value creation by technology. Through the omnipresence of technological innovation, there will always be a technological driver to improve the specific application of a product or service in a market that it was not originally developed for. Any movement from the bottom left to the bottom right will automatically feel the upward pull from technology.

Continuous technological innovation sets in motion an interaction between technology application and market- and organizational change. Interaction that creates meaningful value in a funnel-shaped area in the matrix. In the following chapters, I will explain each of the three stages in the matrix.

CHAPTER 7
Plateau 1: Optimize

Do what you already did,
using more data

H uman beings tend to dislike change. We are 'in the habit of having habits.' Habits offer predictability and thus security. Disturb people in their daily routines and they will get grumpy. In times of economic malaise, the popular vote goes to those who promise to take us 'back to the good old days.' Even John F. Kennedy, in his 1962 historic speech announcing the Apollo space program and the intention to put a man on the moon, mentioned that for many Americans the speed of change was so high that they "…would have us stay where we are a little longer. To rest, to wait." Change, after all, is risky and tiring. As for human beings, for business change is difficult. Although to achieve growth businesses are, by their nature, willing to accept the 'tiring' bit, they are very hesitant about the 'risky' part.

In business, innovation is a paradox. Businesses are most profitable when they operate in a steady environment in which all processes can be optimized for maximum efficiency. Change introduces switching costs and learning costs and wreaks havoc on efficiency. Change is good, but only if it makes doing what we already did more efficient.

It is not surprising, then, that innovative technology in most organizations is initially regarded as a great way to improve efficiency. In my experience, the clear majority of digital technology projects in large organizations are not initiated because of their potential to innovate, but because of their potential to save money and increase speed. They are aimed at what I call 'doing what you always did, using more data.'

Optimizing efficiency is by no means a bad thing. On the contrary, many examples show that analytics of existing data can contribute to great improvements and additional revenue.

One of the most obvious examples of such improvement is consumer analytics. Marketers especially are interested in analyzing consumer behavior with the intent to better target potential customers, convert them faster into paying customers and better serve existing ones. Before the era of analytics, such analysis was difficult and, in some cases, even impossible.

Analytics now holds the promise to solve a problem as old as the marketing profession itself.

To this very day, marketers around the world describe this problem by quoting American entrepreneur John Wanamaker who, in the early 20th century, stated that "...half the money I spend on advertising is wasted; the trouble is I don't know which half". By today's standards, it is more likely that 70-80% of marketing communication is outright ignored by consumers and might as well not have been placed. The classic answer is to place more intrusive ads in more locations. Consumers are clearly not having it and the effect is minimal. Analytics offers a promising answer to this situation. By collecting data from websites, apps, in-store sensors, and a host of other sources, data scientists are able to extract individual behavior and respond with ads and offers with personalized messages, decimating wasted ad-spend and minimizing the negative strain on consumers.

Digital technology can, almost literally, work miracles on existing business problems and inefficiencies. The value of analytics, in particular, allows organizations to very quickly achieve significant improvements in existing processes. From an innovation perspective, Plateau 1 initiatives are often regarded as inferior. They are 'sustaining innovations,' 'mere improvements' of existing business and therefore perhaps not as interesting as true breakthrough innovations. But in reality, Plateau 1 initiatives, because of their proximity to existing business, have a far greater likelihood to offer tangible success. They offer a very rapid feedback cycle from an existing and mature market and from that a stream of data to adjust and improve. Exactly here lies the Jekyll and Hyde of Plateau 1: although it is the easiest plateau to achieve success in, such success also reinforces the hurdle to move to Plateau 2 and to develop a culture of continuous innovation.

Key principles of Plateau 1

Plateau 1 is recognizable by three key principles which describe both the success and risk of digital innovation:

- Innovations reinforce existing targets
- Success stimulates a tendency to over-optimize
- Success creates managerial distance from innovation

Innovations reinforce existing targets

When I worked with a large publisher on implementing data-driven innovations, my team developed two specific analytics programs: the first program used analysis of reading patterns of site visitors to predict the click-ratio on banner advertisements. Banner ads were paid for by advertisers based on the number of clicks, rather than on the number of views. If the newspaper could increase the click-ratio, not only would the advertiser spend more money on ads, the publisher could serve more banners for different advertisers.

Rather than predetermining which banner to show to a given audience, we developed an algorithm that analyzed reading behavior before people who had clicked a banner. The algorithm would then automatically present the banner to a specific user that would be most likely to be clicked by him or her, based on previously read articles. We would ask advertisers to provide us with five different banners and showed each banner to 10,000 visitors. The system analyzed the banner clicks of this group and then determined the likelihood of each banner to be clicked by the next visitor, based on his or her reading behavior. The banner with the highest probability would be served and the response analyzed and added to the calculation for the next consumer. Using this algorithm, banner clicks, and thus the publishers' income, in some cases went up by as much as 800%. It was doing exactly what was already being done, only smarter, by using more data.

The second program was aimed at increasing the conversion ratio of new website visitors to paying subscribers of the print edition of the newspaper. By analyzing the reading patterns of each individual visitor, we were able to provide him or her with an offer based on their preferences. People who had read a significant number of articles from the economics and finance section were offered a subscription including access to premium online articles, a daily newsletter on economics, and the weekend edition of the print newspaper. The banner message was targeted at businesspeople offering to keep them "always up to date when on the road and relaxed during the weekends." People with a particular interest in sports, however, received an offer promising them to be "the first to hear the latest scores throughout the week and in-depth match analyses during weekends." Conversion rates went up by as much as 400%.

Plateau 1 leverages innovative technology which is relatively easy to understand and deploy and which is aimed at improving in existing markets within existing organizational structures and boundaries. The two example projects at the publisher (and four more like it) were realized simultaneously in just under 16 weeks.

The key to success lied in the fact that the results contributed directly to the existing targets and KPIs of the marketing and ad-sales departments. Also, the required technological changes had a minimal impact on the existing process of selling banners or placing ads for subscriptions. And not in the least, all six projects targeted existing customers in existing markets. We were not selling anything new. We were selling the same thing more effectively.

From a technology perspective, we started by not using any specific technology at all. The teams that ran the projects consisted of marketers, managers, database experts, and salespeople. They used their existing knowledge and existing systems during what was called a SWICH (Six Week Innovation CHallenge). For six weeks per project, one day per week, the team would use its combined expertise and insights to draw up a short-term plan, collect the data from existing systems, using existing tools and an overdose of optimism and drive. Within 2 weeks the team would have produced a 'Minimum Viable Product', or MVP, which they could test in real life. The MVP was *Minimum* in the sense that it still required a lot of tasks to be performed manually, such as the selection of target users and placement of the algorithm on specific test pages. It was *Viable*, because the results it returned were no test-cases, they were live results from the actual website and the conversions were for real paying customers and advertisers. Once tested, the team would analyze the results and build improvements into the next version of the product.

The take-away from the examples above is that projects leveraging innovative technology have two key components that need to be optimized and balanced simultaneously: technology and organization. The success of the publisher example lies in the fact that the project never aimed to implement technology or revolutionize the organization. It carefully used an abundance of unused data to improve an existing process with minimal change. The changes were orchestrated by people already working on the subjects and with the technology. They focused on commercial result, rather than on implementing a change. They improved the offering of existing products to existing customers. They had found a way to achieve their existing targets in a more sophisticated way. Already experts in their field, they became even better at what they were doing.

Successful innovations over-optimize

Once proven successful, digital innovations have a tendency to scale-up and expand without becoming more innovative. Management, convinced by its earlier return on investment, will support (or even order) a broader application of the new technology in an attempt to achieve even more efficiency.

Although this may seem logical at first, it may not be as straight forward as it appears. Moving 'up' from Plateau 1 in the matrix means investing in (relatively) more complex technology to achieve more efficiency in something the organization was already doing. Assuming there is a large margin for optimization at the beginning, this margin will shrink as the initial investments pay off. Moving up, however, also means introducing more complex technology and with it more complex management, training, and costs. Moving up essentially means chasing a decreasing margin potential at increasing costs.

In addition, another problem may arise when improving the existing offerings. Plateau 1 changes tend to move not only up, but right, influencing the organization's processes. In the publisher example, processes changed because sales representatives, sponsored content editors, and customers started interacting far more often to discuss campaign results and new targets. Scaling up Plateau 1 initiatives (or adding 'more of the same') often ignores these rightward movements and frequently diminishes the positive effects required to move from Plateau 1 to Plateau 2.

Success creates managerial distance from innovation

At this point, two important 'cultural' factors come into play: resistance to change and something that I call 'managerial distance.' Both factors limit the potential of innovative technology and make it even harder to substantiate the cost and complexity of innovative technology.

When moving up the matrix from Plateau 1, complexity of technology increases, and with it, the changes required in the existing operational processes. In the example of the publisher, sales reps need to sell more complex targeted advertising services to advertisers and marketers need to offer more differentiated subscriptions. Some salespeople will feel as if their sales pitches are replaced by algorithms and their 'market experience' being disputed by overzealous data scientists. With increasing complexity comes an increasing impact on the organization and its habits. And with it the first signs of the 'gravitational pull' of datafication. The result, inevitably, is resistance to change.

A second impacting factor in moving upwards is an increase in 'managerial distance.' When innovative technology projects kick-off, management support is often just around the corner. Innovative technology is risky and fun and attracts management attention for both reasons. But when initial results prove satisfactory and the intricacies of technology become more common knowledge, management often (and understandably) will take more distance and trust on the technology to 'do its magic.'

This increased distance in management attention brings with it a delay in understanding that the technology exerts increasing pressure on the organization to 'move right.' Technology allows for smarter ways of working and additional features and services, but only when the organization changes to new processes. For example, sales representatives selling different products and subscriptions to new personalized products and new processes to deliver them.

Many times, these new processes require crossing existing organizational and managerial boundaries. Increased managerial distance throughout this phase leads to a lack of commitment and understanding of technological innovation. Being attuned to the traditional paradigm of data as an enabler of business (rather than the driver of business), managers often try hard to 'maintain focus' and 'not get carried away.' More often than not, the potential for innovative change is regarded a threat to the status quo and further development is frustrated by a stringent managerial focus on existing KPIs and targets.

UPS: Right hand turns only

One striking example of 'doing what you already did using more data' comes from United Parcel Service (UPS). The US-based parcel delivery service is heavily reliant on efficiency to turn a good profit. UPS operates over 100,000 vehicles for the delivery of parcels. Each vehicle makes approximately 120 deliveries per day. Even a small improvement in each delivery results in massive savings and as a consequence, in profit. Saving just one mile per driver per day results in a US$50 million saving per year. That is why, in 2003, UPS started working on a system called Orion (On-Road Integrated Optimization and Navigation).

Orion is an algorithm and software application analyzing vast amounts of data from delivery vans, traffic, and geographic information systems to calculate the most efficient routes possible while still making deliveries on time. In 2017, Orion saved up to seven or eight miles per truck, resulting in a US$400 million cost saving compared to 2003. This includes savings on time, fuel, rubber, vehicle damages, and an impressive 100,000 metric tons of CO_2 emissions per year.

Orion's algorithms weren't built overnight. Since 2003, the team of developers, data scientists and support staff has grown to 700 people. Indeed, the algorithm has changed significantly through new insights and experience, and with it, UPS's modus operandi for planning and scheduling deliveries and trucks. Orion set out as a system to optimize deliveries bases on allotted delivery time and destination per parcel. Shaving off miles was the dominant goal, and analytics were the tool.

Orion and its developers continuously optimize routes and are experimenting with and finding new variables to optimize profit and customer satisfaction. Such variables originate from suggestions for improvement offered by the algorithms through pattern recognition in the data and from creative reasoning from data scientists, who prove their idea using analytics.

One of the more eccentric ideas that turned out to be a true cost-saver was the idea that making right-hand turns was likely cheaper than making left-hand turns. A right-hand turn most likely uses less gasoline, since a right-hand turn covers less distance than a left-hand turn, and consequently the van accelerates a shorter period of time and burns less fuel. For the same reason, the tires experience less wear and tear and in addition right-hand turns only cross one lane of traffic, decreasing the chance of accidents compared to left-hand turns crossing at least two lanes of traffic. Even though the cost savings per day may not seem like much when extrapolated to

100,000 vehicles each doing hundreds of turns every day, the effect is amplified over many millions of turns.

Obviously, these benefits would have to weigh up against additional costs in terms of time and distance when no left-hand turns were allowed. Orion went to work, analyzing the difference in thousands of routes using left and right-hand turns versus right-hand turns only. The results were astounding: 'right-hand turns only' had the potential to save millions of dollars, and Orion was programmed to calculate routes with as many right-hand turns as possible.

Orion caused its own shift in thinking about efficiency at UPS. As it turned out, Orion's ground-breaking analytics capability to optimize performance might well have had disastrous consequences had the team not recognized the opportunities for new processes and services in time.

Orion's optimization algorithms are based on straightforward principles and process steps. Suppose a parcel has no specific delivery time, Orion might well suggest it would be most efficient for UPS to drop it off at the end of a route, at the end of the day. By doing so, Orion offers the most efficient routes per day, and save significant mileage and thus costs. However, UPS data scientists and managers found out that distance and time are not the only important variables. Many recipients of parcels are businesses. If a business usually receives its packages in the morning, processes them, and sends a reply to its customers the same day, that business will not be pleased to receive the parcel only late in the day. It will have no time left to attend to the package and respond to the customer that same day. Delivering the parcel in the evening may be most cost-efficient for UPS, but certainly not for its customer. Moreover, it would likely cost UPS money when customers could not send return packages the same day. Predictability turned out to be as important for clients as time and destination.

To deal with this situation, Orion's data scientists now needed more data to determine when clients were expecting to have their parcel delivered. One way to obtain this data was by analyzing historical data: trying to discover whether clients who received packages in the morning were more likely to send new packages later that day. However, while this analysis showed a correlation, this still did not shed any light on customer preferences. Nor did it guarantee a higher turnover. After all, if the algorithm determined that certain businesses required delivery in the morning, there was no way to tell if the added costs for plotting a suboptimal route outweighed the potential additional revenue.

A different solution was needed. UPS reverted to what, in The New Oil, I called the principle of 'reciprocity.' It created a new data-driven product which, through its use, generated new unique data from customers. The product in question was MyChoice, an easy to use online tool which notified customers of pending deliveries and allowed them to change delivery times based on their availability. MyChoice proved an excellent solution. It generated a wealth of insights into customer preferences and allowed for true customer-centric delivery routes. As a bonus, it greatly reduced the number of failed delivery attempts and it turned a healthy profit: over seven million customers signed up for the service and are willing to pay up to US$5 per change or US$40 annually for unlimited changes.

MyChoice could have been built without Orion. Yet without MyChoice, Orion would have remained a Plateau 1 innovation for UPS: doing what the company always did, using more data. The realization of UPS's data scientists that, through Orion, the company could discover and market new products and leverage new processes formed the uplift to Plateau 2: new processes in exiting business. The Orion program and the MyChoice product are a point in case of the gravitational pull of data-driven innovation. Both are a success from a technological point as much as from an organizational point of view. The fact that the Orion program is a business responsibility developed in close cooperation with UPS's CIO office was pivotal to that success.

CHAPTER 8
Plateau 2: Transform

Leverage new processes in your existing business

Sometime during the late 1990's I learned one of the most valuable lessons in digital transformation, and I still pass it on to my clients. I was involved in a project for an organization named ZON, which aimed to bring the Internet to the agricultural wholesale and auction house.

Established in 1915, ZON had essentially operated the same processes for over a century. Although most of the administrative processes had been effectively automated and ZON was regarded as a 'modern' organization, the original rhythm of crop growers bringing in their produce in the morning, ready to sell it at auction that same day and then ship it out to buyers, had remained the core activity of the organization throughout time.

I was member of team that had developed a new intranet system that would give growers online access to their supply statistics and save the auctioneer the hassle of administering all of the delivered goods at the moment of delivery during an already hectic first two hours of the day. The business case of our new Intranet, I was convinced, was in speed and fault reduction. I was about to learn why, in the 'Internet Age,' that would not work.

In walked a tall man in his late forties, named Tony. He was the newly-appointed program manager overseeing the digitization of ZON. When we sat down to discuss my ideas about the process, Tony leaned back and said, "I see what you mean." And then there was an uncomfortable silence. After a moment or two, Tony stood up and said, "I'll write down a rule I live by, and that has helped me a great deal in avoiding mistakes. Keep this in the back of your head at all times." He walked to a whiteboard, picked up a marker and wrote:

Old Processes X New Technology = Expensive Operations

When he put down the marker, Tony discovered he had used a permanent marker to write on the whiteboard. His valuable lesson turned out to be non-removable. "Never mind," he said with a smile, "it is a lesson for everyone to learn."

Tony's lesson is the best explanation for what I called the 'gravitational pull' of datafication. Whenever an organization implements new, innovative technology, it is bound to have an impact on its existing processes. If it doesn't, either the existing processes are hideously inefficient, or (more likely) the efficiency increase achieved by the new technology is relatively small compared to its cost.

Innovative technology allows organizations to find innovative ways to solve customer problems. It offers an opportunity to break free from the limitations of existing solutions to add inherent value. It allows us to review the original problem and find creative ways to solve it, rather than incremental changes to the existing solution. Although this sounds self-evident, organizations and individuals have tremendous difficulties in putting that theory to practice.

When the Internet became popular in the late 1990s, many newspaper publishers found that online technology offered a new way to publish news. They excitedly launched their first websites and copied articles from the print editions to the online version, thinking that's all there was to it. I can vividly remember how one of the first online newspapers even stuck to the column-based layout in the online edition of its paper, requiring readers to scroll up and down when switching from column to column.

Although these sorts of mistakes were common and quickly corrected, most newspapers had tremendous difficulty in realizing that their online editions had no need for a publishing deadline. Paper-based newspapers required a process in which news articles were written and collected until a particular time of day (i.e., the deadline), when all articles were combined into a single edition which was sent off to the printer, printed, and distributed to readers. The online version had no need to wait for a deadline: the newspaper was online 24/7 and there was no printing process or distribution system to adhere to. Yet the existing processes in most newsrooms did not allow for the immediate publication of articles; editors worked not at a pace for immediate publication but for meeting a distant deadline.

Other types of news publishers (for instance, television-based news channels like CNN) were much better equipped to adapt to this new technology, and they gained ground over their paper-based competitors. Television processes were better prepared to 'scoop' the news, but many of them were not equipped to deliver written content. Despite this challenge, news broadcasters realized (far quicker than printed media) that the internet offered them a great means to overcome the limitations of broadcast television. Using the new opportunities that innovative technology offered them, broadcasters extended their market share in the news industry quickly and efficiently.

The technology-driven transformation of the media industry did not end there. Innovative technology has not only affected the distribution side of news media. It has impacted news consumption altogether. It has changed consumer behavior in an impressive way. Today, for consumers, news is as much a way to stay informed as it is a way to fight boredom. And consumers have become editors themselves by providing comments to news and even scoops, such as through Twitter, and complete news articles.

This change has had an even greater impact on the competitive position of newspapers than anything else. Not so much because it allowed competitors to offer a product or service that newspapers could not offer, but because the new behavior of consumers simply did not match the existing processes and 'modus operandi' of traditional publishers. A combination of reluctance to change in editorial teams and an inability to invest in change in a declining market is quickly putting publishers in a downward spiral.

Plateau 2 and the 'glass ceiling'

Remember the newspaper case from the previous chapter? When the Big Data analytics projects started, the publisher had been in choppy commercial waters for some time. Subscription rates had been dropping steadily and the company had been losing money over several consecutive years. The online product of the company was outdated, and the development of new online propositions was floundering.

The company management looked at data as a new source of income and a driver for new business models. The program focused on building consumer behavioral profiles. The publisher offered its readers a national newspaper with a number of popular editorial sections about finance, sports, lifestyle, and in addition a selection of regional publications and special interest websites. Because of this, the audience was large, visitor frequency was high, and the potential of collectible data was huge. Therefore, there existed great potential to create individual visitor profiles about content preference and interests, geographic location, socio-demographic information, and income classification.

Despite its financial difficulties, the company was in a great position to build a detailed overview of consumer profiles. Using these profiles, the company could offer more personalized products and services, including paid services (as opposed to the existing 'free' offering, supported by advertisements) to consumers. In addition, it could increase the price of advertisements through offering the placement of advertisements to specifically targeted consumer groups and it could offer more tailored subscription plans to printed news media. Beyond those possibilities, new data-driven business models based on leveraging consumer profiles looked both innovative and promising.

As soon as the project got underway, it became clear that placing focus on consumer behavior was incompatible with the existing processes. These processes emphasized not consumers but content areas, such as news, sports, or lifestyle. The differences were many.

Some of the content teams were simply more interested in their specific topics than in consumer segments. Some editorial teams were racing towards weekly deadlines for glossy magazines, others for daily deadlines or immediate scoops. The advertising sales department did not typically sell targeted advertisements but focused on offering the largest widespread reach in the country. Subscription sales and call center agents focused on selling a single product in multiple subscription plans, not towards multiple products with a single, simple subscription plan. And to top it all, everyone in the company felt the pressure of the increasing losses and rigorous targets for improvement set by management.

Every step out of the ordinary was considered a threat to meeting those targets. The data program, people argued, was a great idea, as long as it did not interfere with their current operations. But of course, it did. The program required people to change their view of what exactly the company was selling. It required people from different departments to synchronize their actions and campaigns. To make the program work, changes to websites and apps would be required. And disparate IT systems would have to be aligned.

When launched, the program was met with great enthusiasm from nearly all employees and management. The CEO himself initiated the program, senior management applauded it, and funding was secured easily. The program plan even pointed clearly to the impact of data on the existing organizational structure. Everyone agreed is should be changed if the program required it. People were excited when the first pilot results came in better than expected. Then, six months underway in the program, the data program was handed over to the business teams, much earlier than planned. The program, as it was reasoned, was a success and now 'the business' should take responsibility and scale-up.

In itself, it may have been a commendable decision to hand responsibility for the program to the business. But management failed to acknowledge that many existing processes had not been changed. Business targets, key performance indicators, teams, responsibilities, and culture technically remained as they were six months earlier. Sure, there were pilot teams that had performed proofs-of-concept. Over 60 highly motivated people had worked part-time in small, multidisciplinary teams, realizing data-driven goals. But as soon as the 'project' became the responsibility of the core organization, the business looked at how these activities contributed to their operational KPI's.

Within several weeks after the transition to the business, managers assigned the project's team members back to their original duties, helping to reach the same, non-data-driven targets as before. With one exception: the advertising sales team did manage to create and sell a 'targeted ads' proposition and significantly increase its profit margin on placed ads. A performance metric that had been in place since the company started selling ads, a century before.

By today, most of the promising data-driven initiatives have come to a halt. Without any manager actively putting an end to them. They were not actively stopped, but the project's activities lacked an organizational anchor and were simply not pursued anymore. They did not hit a 'brick wall' but rather a 'glass ceiling.' A classic transformational boundary, yet a significantly powerful force: resistance to change. Several people have written books about how organizations can overcome this resistance, and it is not the aim of this book to add to that volume. However, it is important to realize that at the end of Plateau 1, change is inevitable.

Key principles of Plateau 2

In Plateau 1, digital technology and data enable existing processes, in Plateau 2 data and its accompanying technologies become an integral part of them. In Plateau 2, data does not facilitate the process, but *drives* it; the process cannot be performed without the data. This leads to three key organizational issues:

- Processes and KPIs will change
- Organizational silos will break
- Multidisciplinary teams will be required

Processes and KPIs change

An organization is essentially a collection of processes performed by dedicated teams and individuals. In order to manage the organization, each process is continually adjusted or "tuned" to perform as optimally as possible. This performance is measured by Key Performance Indicators (KPIs). Since each process is managed by a responsible person, the KPIs not only measure the effectiveness of a process but, implicitly, also that of that person. Add a pinch of corporate politics and powerplay, and implicit becomes explicit: KPIs indicate personal effectiveness.

In Plateau 2, data changes an existing process; this impacts both the performance of the process and the measurement of its KPIs. Since the KPIs were modeled after the 'old' process, they are likely to not correctly show the effectiveness of the 'new' process. As a result, the responsible person often has some explaining to do to his superiors about why results are not as expected. Tuning the old operational process to the new process is one thing. Adjusting KPIs, including task descriptions, managerial reach and responsibilities, and technological dependencies, is an even more difficult task. Breaking the glass ceiling is not a matter of proving that data-driven initiatives deliver more value, it is a matter of being able to change organizational responsibilities and the way in which they are measured.

Silos will break

Throughout the years, incumbent organizations have been organized around markets and product groups. Most corporations have traditionally optimized their organizational structures to create maximum efficiency for each task in their value chains. In this model, the R&D department develops a product, procurement purchases parts, production joins them together, marketing promotes the product, sales closes the deal, and service installs and provides aftercare.

Before the digital age, most new products would fit neatly into this structure. Digital products and services and data analytics, however, have a nasty habit of breaking molds.

Utility providers found out the hard way when solar panels gained popularity in Europe and smart meters were introduced. When legislation forced utility providers to buy energy produced by private individuals' solar panels at the same price at which they sold energy to them, their business models simply became irrelevant. This was because their models were built around the procurement of energy from a few large producers, not hundreds of thousands of small ones (and especially not at the price point that they were forced to observe).

Another reason why organizational silos break is that data from digital products can be used to analyze a customer's usage of a product in real-time. Such analysis provides immediate feedback about the product quality and features, and the customer's preferences, and can either steer user behavior or change the product characteristics.

For instance, websites from airlines monitor visitor's search behavior for flights. Whenever return visitors search for a particular destination over the course of multiple days, the site may return higher prices for tickets, assuming the prospective buyer is more interested in that ticket when he returns more often. Such predetermined actions require extensive cooperation between employees of the airline in product development, pricing, web development, sales, and planning.

User data from various digital products (including cell phones, cars, connected home appliances, websites, apps, and social media) all provide companies with insights to how their customers use their services. This makes it possible to segment customer groups not only by socio-demographic factors (e.g., business users vs. private individuals) but by users' actual behavior.

This type of 'cross-silo' analytics is usually propagated by data enthusiasts in the organization as early as Plateau 1 and usually delivers many new insights. However, it requires applying the new segments in a structural way in marketing and product management and collaboration with partner companies. This quite often leads to some very practical problems in existing organizational structures. The new capabilities brought on by data not only require new expertise in terms of understanding data and technology. They also require the ability to break free from organizational conventions and silos.

Multidisciplinary teams will be required

Traditionally, asset-centric organizations focus on optimizing risk management and operational efficiency. The paradigm being that tangible, capital intensive assets represent a rare and expensive competitive means to create predictable output of value. People are organized to create maximum efficiency around those tools.

In data-driven organizations, things tend to be the other way around: data is ubiquitous, fluid, and short-lived. Insights into current developments enable a transition from steady, predictable processes to fast, situational dependent processes. In this sort of situation, people are ideally organized for speed and adaptability rather than for efficiency.

The most popular way to organize such capability is through adopting an Agile way of working. In Agile working, teams of people with often different but complementary skills set out to complete tasks in short iterations. Each team will create a working solution in each iteration. Rather than handing off partial work to the next team, each team is responsible for creating and maintaining end-to-end working solutions.

In this system, instead of a team of product managers requesting a report from a team of data analysts somewhere in the IT department in order to instruct a team of web developers to design and maintain a new webpage, a small team consisting of a product manager, analysts, and web developers becomes responsible for the entire process in close cooperation. Such a multidisciplinary team is capable of delivering targeted value much faster than traditionally organized departments.

Data and its accompanying technology have made it possible to better respond to change. However, most organizations are not equipped to support this change to multidisciplinary teams and Agile working. In innovation strategy, Plateau 2 takes center stage when it comes to adopting *new processes in existing businesses*.

Plateau 2 is the magnet for change

Why is it important to change the organization to enable new data- and technology-driven products and services? What if we would use data solely to optimize for efficiency? The simple answer is that moving straight upward in the model from Plateau

1 is a dead end. Efficiency is achieved by investing more money in data collection, processing, and analytical technology. Eventually, adding more technology will not create more financial advantage and the investments net result will become negative. But there is a more compelling reason: Plateau 2 works like a magnet. Data allows organizations to create new services and solutions that range well beyond their existing propositions. Organizations will not be able to deliver these services and solutions without changing their processes and organizational structure. Once competitors start offering new types of solutions in the marketplace, there will be no way to ignore the new standard.

The Financial Times' team would not have able to serve specifically targeted online advertisements without adapting its sales approach and without tuning its web development team to personalized web pages. Once Yahoo! Finance started using analytics as a driver for ad-effectiveness, there was no way back for any online publisher. A similar example has taken place in e-commerce with the launch of 'same-day delivery' services. In this case, data did not just create a compelling case for changing processes. It spurred the development of something called *'anticipatory shipping,'* which is propelling an entire industry to rethink its business models and enter Plateau 3.

As early as 2014, two US-based retailers – Gilt.com and Amazon.com – had independently started experimenting with data analytics to reduce the delivery time of the goods sold on their websites.

High-end fashion retailer Gilt.com aimed to start transferring garments from regional warehouses to local distribution centers even before they were sold, based on the statistical probability of a customer buying those garments in the next few days in that region. By the time the clothes are actually purchased, they are geographically closer to the customer and the customer will get them faster. By optimizing this process, goods can be delivered the same day they are ordered while Gilt.com keeps less local stock, reducing costs. Gilt.com expects that future delivery times may be reduced even further by sending trucks out into neighborhoods with products still unpacked, only to box them when the order has been made and deliver them within an hour of ordering.

Amazon.com takes anticipatory shipping one step beyond shipping items early in the logistical chain. Amazon has begun to deliver products to clients' doorsteps without them even having ordered them. If the client does not want them, Amazon will pick them up at no cost. If the client decides to keep the goods, Amazon will bill them afterward. It would be easy to regard anticipatory shipping as the next level in logistics, but in fact, it requires a fundamental rethink of the business models for Amazon.com and the vendors they serve.

CHAPTER 9
Plateau 3: Innovate

Even when change is the norm, data flow is remarkably constant

Continuous innovation is about creating sustainable and significant value. Sustainability is important for repetitive and scalable value. Significance here means that the value is aligned with the core mission of the organization. In the vast majority of organizations, adding a digital layer on top of existing strategy is simply too much of distraction from the highly competitive core business.

A few years ago, while working on a project for a large electricity provider, an enthusiastic team of developers and data scientist asked me to join their product demo. The team operated as an 'in-house' startup and was responsible for developing and marketing an innovative online product. In line with the Agile way of working the team had adopted, the product demo showcased the progress the team had made over the previous two weeks. The demo was attended by nearly 35 people, including the team, its product owner, and many business stakeholders who had an interest in the services the team was developing.

During the demonstration, the team proudly announced that it had quadrupled its revenue stream from US$1.25 million to close to US$6 million in the last 24 months. Covered by the roaring applause from their colleagues, one of the VP's of the company smiled to me and mumbled, "I don't know whether to laugh or to cry."

When I asked him for an explanation he said, "Don't get me wrong, the data team is doing a great job. The thing is, if their growth is linear, it will take them exactly eleven years to outperform our smallest business unit, in which case I need to sell off their unit as soon as possible." He paused for second and then continued: "However, if their growth is exponential, they'll have crossed the 75 million mark in 36 months, disrupt our business model and I will be stuck with 300 employees in various other departments who have the wrong education and skills."

The VP made a remarkably good point. Growing beyond Plateau 2 requires more than scaling up a different process. Beyond Plateau 2, technology has the potential not only to change the way your company is organized, but also the markets in which it operates, and the way business is done. One common practice is to create 'stepping stones' to future options. This means to support, create, or take shares in multiple small, often high-risk initiatives that *may* lead to future growth. These are valid strategies indeed, but as the VP illustrated in his remark, digital technology has a nasty habit of sometimes scaling exponentially fast. Stepping stones may well disrupt their parents so quickly that the incumbent's core business is left outpaced and vulnerable.

There is a popular mantra in selling digital transformation to board members: 'Disrupt yourself before someone else does it.' I find such remarks misplaced heroics. First of all, I believe that only markets can be disrupted – not organizations. Organizations, when poorly managed, fail as a result of market disruption, or thrive on it when managed successfully.

But even when presuming the narrative is correct and organizations can 'disrupt themselves,' disrupting oneself is actually a bad thing. It is the willing destruction of value and capital invested. Moreover, it rides on the assumption that *changing* the old is not possible at sufficient speed and that radical measures are required.

If the Agile movement has taught us anything over the last decade, it is that rapid change is not only feasible, it is so successful that it is becoming the norm in organizational strategy. Compared to disruption, controlled rapid change is much more effective.

It should be clear, however, that controlled rapid change is something different than evolutionary development. This is exactly the pitfall that most incumbents encounter when dealing with industry-wide digital disruption. Evolution leads to 'improving what you always did using more data.' It keeps organizations locked in Plateau 1. The key to success with controlled, rapid change is something I call 'continuous innovation'. If the world around our organization changes ever faster, and if our (digital) competitors require less and less capital and time to create potentially disrupting improvements or alternatives to our products, our primary competitive advantage lies in the data we own or can access. From Plateau 2 onwards, organizations must adapt not only to new processes, they need to be able to recognize the possibility and potential for digital, data-driven business models and organize for their fast, effective execution.

Traditionally, the size and structure of corporate organizations brought resilience to change, and with it, resilience to risk. Corporations have typically thrived on efficiency, predictability, and control, which made sense for markets that changed slowly, with grand changes arriving over decades.

Organizational design adapts to the structure of markets; in slow markets, robust organizations work just fine. Organizational form can be thought of as the spine of an organization, optimizing activities across a specific business domain or core competence, thereby creating efficiency and oversight.

Retailers, for instance, mostly organize all outlets in the same way, replicating best practices in logistics, replenishment, store-operations, and administration. The advantages are clear, but when the organization is challenged by change, such as a home delivery service, the current organization is no longer sufficient. Logistics are different, order picking is a new discipline, administration is different since customers pay up-front rather than after delivery. In times of rapid change, the very organizational structure which provided a solid backbone for efficiency and control can quickly turn into an obstruction to adaptation. In heavily digitized markets, change is constant; entry barriers are virtually non-existent, and competition relies on creativity much more than on execution power. Take, for instance, the market for leasing cars.

Across the US and Europe, corporate leasing of cars is big business. The US market for the leasing of business cars alone is worth more than US$2 billion annually. Traditionally, leasing companies are managed as a financial services organization and are usually owned by banks. Their service is in investing upfront in an expensive good, such as a car, and then having the customer pay back the investment including margin over a set period of time, usually a few years.

The lease business is about optimizing the return on investment in capital intensive goods, such as cars, aircraft or agricultural equipment and machinery. It is easy to assume that the people driving the cars are the clients of lease companies, but they are not. Fleet managers are the customers actually paying the bill. Fleet managers look for the best financial deal on the contract for the entire fleet of cars that a company leases, minimizing the monthly financial burden on their organization.

Drivers are often regarded as a necessary inducement to supply the car to, but, since they are not the paying customer, are considered irrelevant otherwise to both fleet owners and leasing companies. So, on the whole, lease companies are organized to deliver the highest ROI in investments, with driver service being a cost center. Digital technology, however, is about to shred this notion to bits by placing the focus on providing means for mobility. In my consulting practice, exactly that was the aim of an intensive digital transformation project that not only introduced new innovative technology to the company, but also changed its organizational structure altogether.

When Jack, CIO of a multinational car leasing company, approached me to help out on the digital transformation of his organization, he knew he was going to have to reinvent his entire organization, not just its systems. Jack had joined the company only recently but was well aware of the recent surge in digitally-powered mobility services such as ride-sharing, mobility services (combining car rental with various types of public transport), and corporate Uber-like services.

The quick rise of such digital services, Jack realized, had led many corporate clients to rethink their mobility strategies. After all, if employees could travel inefficiently organized combinations of transport that also saved on CO_2-emmissions, why would corporations want to bother with long term lease contracts for individual vehicles? Especially in densely populated areas with high parking costs and traffic jams, even the corporation's employees regard lease cars as an expensive nuisance rather than a perk. Add to this the added tax that employees in many countries are required to pay for using a car provided by their employer, and mobility services (usually tax-less) quickly become a sensible and attractive option.

Jack and I pondered the developments of the corporate lease market for the coming five to ten years. We talked to industry veterans and mobility start-ups, we read research papers and market analyses and debated what we read with a team of colleagues and even shareholders.   The corporate car-lease market in Europe, we concluded, will change rapidly from the financial management of investments in automobiles for corporate fleet managers into the delivery of flexible mobility services to end-users. Fleet managers will become 'mobility managers,' delivering the most employee-friendly combination of services, including video-conferencing and flexible workspace offerings. Services will be based on personal budgets per employee and pay-per-use systems will take precedence over negotiating contracts for collections of cars. However, we also noted, neither fleet managers nor mobility managers will oversee the total offering of mobility services in the market. They will not likely be able to negotiate the best deal with each supplier and then combine these offerings into a single, interconnected system for employees. As we progressed, we started drawing the outlines of the new business model for a mobility service provider.

Jack's organization was currently optimized to achieve maximum efficiency and operational excellence in the sales and administration of lease contracts for motor vehicles, and in the procurement of these vehicles. It was so optimized for its existing business that the organization operated an ERP software system that could not register any contract without a license plate number and a reference to make and model car. There was no way that 'mobility services' could be made to fit in this system. Both the processes and accompanying systems would have to be completely redesigned and built from scratch.

Jack found his company operating in a digitized market, where new types of mobility services are being developed and marketed almost on a daily basis by hundreds of companies from all over the world. A market in which drivers are well aware of the latest possibilities that are being developed. In order to service the changing market demand, Jack's company would need to be able to provide state-of-the-art digital services as soon as they gain interest from clients. Rather than develop each service himself, Jack wanted to cherry-pick partners and sell such third-party services to his clients in a single 'mobility contract' where clients could pick and choose from a services menu.

To do so, he needed to define the processes and tools in his organization in such a way that it could offer and support an ever-changing array of services to its clients. That meant that there would never be a status quo in services offered. There would never be a moment to fix and optimize processes and tools to achieve financial and risk stability and optimization for a stable set of services.

Unless we could create such a status quo. During our discussions about the design of the processes and systems of a mobility service provider, Jack and I discovered that there are some things that do not change, regardless of the services provided by third parties: the entities that are subject to the service: clients, users, services, features, time. A specific client would always pay for a specific user to use a specific service with a variation of features at a specific time or timeframe. As long as the system could register data about such entities, the company could sell any product or service to anyone without a need to change the system. The only prerequisite was that new products or services would be able to supply data about the entities in the system.

Each time a product or service was used, data would become available from the provisioning system: a car, an app, a travel-card, a bicycle, an RFID-reader, etc. The key to the future of mobility services was not in designing a system that could connect and restructure all third-party systems, but in designing a system that could collect and connect data from all services. On top of such a system should be an analytics engine to analyze the data from a specific user across all of the services used by this user and suggest the next best travel option based on previous behavior and personal preferences.

Competitive advantage would not rely on managing third party services but on the unique capability to analyze and predict user preferences. We realized that, although this sounded very complex, it would be far from impossible to realize using best-of-breed solutions and custom-built components.

Within weeks Jack contracted some of the brightest ERP vendors and developers and started to iteratively design and build the new 'digital backbone' that would support the administration of existing, traditional lease contracts and an array of third-party mobility services. But when it came time to implement the new applications and services, and when trying to adjust processes accordingly, resistance in the organization arose. Shift away from leasing? Data as a product? No single process to optimize for operational excellence? And what about financial and risk stability? Not only did Jack have to reinvent his company's processes and software, he would have to reinvent its culture too.

Plateau 3 requires not only that organizations change their definition of products and services, within the boundaries of their organizational design. It requires them to redesign the organization itself. But which guidelines should a company use to organize itself if its markets and products are open to continuous change? In Plateau 3, not the product/market structure but the data structure of the company becomes key.

The organization will need to be able to adapt quickly to innovation and adapt to such change rather than to become highly efficient at serving the status quo. The ability to harness change is key, and data is the biggest driver for change. As we will see a few pages from now, if your organization's data structure is modeled wisely, data becomes a remarkably stable entity upon which to build innovations.

Key principles of Plateau 3

Plateau 3 is not a final destination or a prescribed state. It is a vision, a goal to strive for. How this goal is formulated differs per industry and organization. It relies, however, on a number of set principles where data is the key ingredient of value creation, rather than current core value drivers, such as patents, expertise, or production capabilities. In Plateau 3, these are not being replaced by data, but data generated through these capabilities will have surpassed them as the primary unit of value. And a fundamental shift in business model perception is required to distill this value.

The key principles of Plateau 3 are:

- Service trumps production
- Platform trumps product
- Data structure trumps organizational structure
- Speed trumps efficiency
- Installed base trumps everything else

Service trumps production

As we have seen before, traditionally organizations were designed to generate maximum utilization of assets. These principles stem from the era where scarcity was the leading economic driving force and investment in expensive goods safeguarded scarcity. Only organizations with the same resources could afford to compete and through operational excellence, companies tried to outperform each other on increasing the return the capital invested.

Digital services effectively did away with those principles. In their book, 'Abundance' (Diamandis, Abundance: The Future Is Better Than You Think, 2012), Peter Diamandis and Steven Kotler show how digital technology provides access and availability of resources to essentially everyone. Books can be produced at virtually no cost by anyone. Music can be recorded and distributed by artists directly, without the involvement of record companies and e-commerce ventures can be run from an ordinary household. Energy, education, healthcare, news, entertainment all become available in abundances and often for free. The principles of abundance pivot economic principles from basing value on scarcity to basing value on universal availability. In this economy value flows away from the start of the value chain (left), where assets reside, to the front of the value chain (right), where data creates abundance.

The principle of service value is not unique to datafication. It has been taught in universities, business self-help guides, and how-to books already for decades. One well-known example of service value is found in ice cream.

You could purchase good-quality vanilla ice cream in a box in any convenience store at something like US$1 per ounce. That same amount of ice cream would cost up to three or four times that price when purchased from an ice cream vendor in a park on a hot summer day. The service markup for the ice cream in that case would be some 400%. That service markup could increase easily to 2000% when the ice cream is served at the Waldorf Astoria or any other high-end hotel in New York.

The service markup is largely justified by narrowing the time and location of purchase. The ice cream vendor in the park can charge the markup because he prevents his buyers from having to go out of the park to a Wall Mart to buy the ice cream and then be stuck with a half-empty box of ice cream after they have eaten it. In a digital world, the value of the service markup can be decided upon by those who have information about the value of the service added. That value is not necessarily just based on time and location.

This anecdote explains the principle very clearly: One day, a young man brought his car to a body shop after it had been slightly dented in a "fender-bender". He asked the mechanic if he could fix the dent and what the cost would be. The mechanic inspected the car and replied, "I believe I can help you out for US$100."

The man agreed to the price, after which the mechanic opened the boot of the car, looked at the dent from the inside and then took a small hammer out of his pocket. With a single, well-directed blow of the hammer, he knocked the dent outwards; with a soft *clunk,* the dent had disappeared completely.

The bodywork had simply popped back into place. "That'll be one hundred dollars," the mechanic said. The man looked astonished and replied, "One hundred dollars!? That just took you 30 seconds. You cannot charge me one hundred dollars for that? I demand a specification of the costs." The mechanic walked to his office, took out a receipt book and scribbled something on the paper. Then he walked back and handed it to the man. "One hundred dollars, specified as you requested," he said. The young man looked at the receipt and read:

Hitting dent with hammer:	US $	5-
Knowing where to hit	US $	95-
Total	**US$**	**100-**

The anecdote points out that, in situations where explicit knowledge can be applied, the value of service may far exceed the value of the product itself. The service provides the context in which products become more valuable. Data and analytics allow you to find and apply this context at almost any imaginable level and drive the total margin value of a product through service.

In the case of The Financial Times and Yahoo! Finance (as described in the beginning of this book), Yahoo! Finance did not serve a better product that FT.com. Its third-party financial news articles proved to be inferior to the articles written by the renowned editorial board of FT.com. However, because the site measured what visitors were after on their website, Yahoo! could tailor the content to its customer's needs.

The product may have been worse, but the context in which it was provided more than compensated for that lack of quality. For Yahoo! Finance, the core product – the article – was considered a cost; the real margin was in providing contextual service.

Similar examples can be found in other industries, such as General Electric, which because of sensor technology and data analytics can now offer its customers predictive maintenance as a service. Such a service represents a steady income model and higher returns per customers, for which customers in return receive less downtime for maintenance and unexpected breakdowns and repairs.

Platform trumps product

In the age of abundance, margin value lies not in owning (scarce) resources, but in operating highly scalable services. If you are a content provider whose data is abundant, an even smarter strategy than operating your own service is providing your data at a minimum cost to third parties and to allow them to build services on this data. After all, if data scales at virtually no cost and others are creative enough to turn your data into multiple value-added services, your best strategy is to charge all of them for using your data rather than to charge customers for the use of your exclusive service. Facilitating abundance is quite profitable.

The key to this business model is the digital platform. The owners of such online platforms can grant data access to third parties, who may build and operate a service based on this data, and who pay a fee for each time the data is used or accessed. Obviously, the type of access (i.e., speed, volume, frequency of access) and additional functionality (analysis and combination of datasets) are controlled by the platform owner and can be charged separately.

For instance, a utility provider selling solar panels to homeowners could launch a platform on which panel owners can view the production of solar energy through their panels. On the same platform, they can allow third parties to develop apps through which homeowners can sell their surplus generated electricity to each-other or trade energy for other products and goods. By allowing third parties to develop such apps, more creativity and more development power come available to the platform. By allowing not just utility clients but anyone with solar panels to connect their panel data to the platform, more data comes available in the platform and the total value of the platform increases for everyone. Value is generated for participating developers through subscriptions or transaction fees and the utility gets a fee for data usage.

Platforms make great sense in Plateau 3 strategies, because
incumbents represent a known and trusted producer to a
relatively large number of data-rich consumers. The incumbent
therefor can kick start the launch a platform with an immediate
installed base of users.

Many great books have already been written about leveraging
platform strategies, so I will not try to go into detail on this topic.
However, in the context of this book, a few things are important
to know about platforms and why they trump products.

1. Platforms operate a two-sided business model
2. Platforms increase the value of physical assets
3. Platforms leverage the success of competitors

Platforms operate a two-sided business model

Platforms sit comfortably in the middle between two dependent
parties: producers and consumers. Producers want to join the
platform because it represents a marketplace for consumers.
Consumers are attracted to the platform because it offers instant
value from a multitude of offerings. Platforms tend to reinforce
themselves when both sides are available in large enough
numbers and in balance.

This effect is referred to as the 'network effect.' Incumbents with
a sizeable installed base of consumers may opt to deliver their
services through a digital platform and provide access to this
platform to third parties with the aim to activate the second side
of the platform business model. In addition to building a
business from providing branded digital services, they can build

a business from charging transaction fees to other producers providing services through the digital platform.

Platforms increase value of physical assets

Any physical product can be extended through digital services by means of a web interface, an app, or extensions to existing online services such as Twitter or Facebook. The added value of the services to the product is limited by the capability (and in practice often the willingness) of the producer to add more services on top of the physical product.

Platforms offer additional advantages. Because the development of services is not limited to the original producer, development capability and creativity attain a global reach. Anyone can build any new service and services may even be stacked on top of existing services. Features and services from other physical products may be linked through the platform to the original product. These kinds of unpredictable development offer not just a myriad of new services to a physical product, they also increase the 'future potential' of that product. The product becomes more valuable because of the increased likelihood that new services can and will be added to it over time.

When Apple first launched its iPhone in 2007, the Apple team itself developed all the available apps; users could not download or install more apps. By 2008, Apple released the iPhone 3G and with it came the 'App Store', the platform for services to be used on the physical iPhone product. On its launch date of July 10th, 2008, the App Store featured 500 apps. Third-party developers were actively encouraged to develop apps and publish them in the App Store. One might argue that Apple could have made far better margins on apps that it developed itself. However, by 2017 the App Store features over 2 million apps that had generated a combined revenue of over US$70 billion for developers. With Apple's margin on average being 30%, the App Store generated over US$20 billion in revenue.

Today, it is obvious that consumers greatly admire the physical technical features of the iPhone, such as its touch screen and sleek design. Yet without the promise of new apps and services, the perceived value of the phone would, without a doubt, have been much smaller.

Platforms leverage success of competitors

Digitization increases competition in incumbent markets because the development of digital value-added services is fast, cheap, and ubiquitous. Barriers to entry are extremely low, especially since Agile and iterative development methods have created a culture that values the immediate release of 'minimum viable products' and their rapid updates and improvements.

In the age of scarcity, producers were rewarded for creating service exclusive to their own physical products ("if you want to enjoy this service you need to buy the original brand X"). In the digital age of abundance, value is in providing services to, and on top of, any competing product, as long as the service is provided through the specific platform. Margin is not made through the sales of the hardware but through the provisioning of services. Why not use competitors' hardware as leverage to sell software?

Caterpillar, the renowned manufacturer of earthmoving and construction equipment, was one of the pioneers in electronic monitoring of vehicles, measuring anything from engine to hydraulic and operation data. Caterpillar quickly recognized the demand for a single online platform in which clients could monitor a fleet of equipment from multiple manufacturers. Rather than enforce Caterpillar exclusivity by keeping the platform closed to Caterpillar vehicles only (using the platform as leverage to steer buying decisions towards Caterpillar equipment), 'Cat' opened up its platform to data from competing makes. The company today even supplies hardware modules to upgrade competitor's machines to send data to the Caterpillar platform, called VisionLink, directly leveraging value from its competitors' turnover in the market.

Data structure trumps organizational structure

In Chapter 4.1, 'Three value drivers for data', I showed that until the end of the twentieth century, organizations primarily generated and used data for administrative purposes. This led to the situation where most of the data collected and stored in organizations, to this day, mirrors the organizational structure of its creator. Databases of sales records or product usage often reflect organizational and process hierarchy because the data was never intended to (or allowed to) be used outside of the organizational context. Many databases were modeled explicitly to provide or limit access to data by specific members of staff.

With time, the data structure of organizations grows deeper and wider and more and more resembles the siloed organizational structure and growth. Since the turn of the 21st century a field of expertise called 'Enterprise Architecture' has emerged to counter such immobility of data, but business management is often difficult to convince to invest in a modern, flexible data architecture at great expense but with only limited tangible short-term value. This struggle is common throughout the practice of innovation.

This idea of data structure vs. organizational structure is illustrated by a project I was involved in some time ago. It involves a car leasing company that organized its database in such a way that the car license plate was the unique identifier for a record. Multiple records were linked to define a client, meaning that the system regarded multiple license plates as a single corporate client. The data design assumed that the business model entailed leasing vehicles to companies. The data was primarily used to calculate invoices.

Then the lease company introduced an app aimed at servicing individual drivers with personalized maintenance schedules and alerts for tire changes. It turned out that the data model of the vehicle administration could not provide the right data for the app. Although it was clear from the start that the data model was at the core of the problem, the issue was regarded as a feature problem and was resolved by building a work-around for the database and by storing temporary copies of the car data in a separate database.

Only a few months after the rework had finished, the company had partnered with a telematics provider, requiring all cars to be fitted with GPS and On-Board Diagnostics-computer, sending masses of car performance data to the partner company, and storing some key figures about car performance and driver behavior in the company system. This time, the problem was reversed; the core database of the company had no way of storing all of this automatically generated data.

Furthermore, a new problem arose: the telematics system automatically provided the mileage figure from each car, but the administrative system could not take the number in, for it had been designed to capture this data whenever the drivers would use their fuel card at a gas station and were required to fill out his/her current mileage as part of the payment process. Before the issue of data synchronization was even resolved, a third problem arose when the lease company wanted to allow car sharing between individual employees of a single client. The lease company had acquired a car-sharing startup to manage the process, but it proved to be impossible to connect the core system to the car-sharing app without slowing the whole administrative system down to the point where it became useless for employees.

The lease company finally decided that there was no alternative but to redevelop the system from the ground up. This time, it did not take its process as a basis for its data design, but it modeled its data after the key entities in the mobility market: clients (both corporate and private), users (explicitly not drivers: who knows, the company might be leasing drones within a few years!), services (apps, reports, alerts, and planning tools), products (cars, public transport, fuel, and rides in driverless cars) and contract (basically describing a particular relationship between any of the entities above).

Now the data could be shared between each and any entity, regardless of whether it was used by employees, clients, users, partners, or things. By decoupling the data structure from the organizational structure, the company in effect created a data platform for mobility. This allowed for virtually limitless partnerships and links to third parties and created flexibility and a capability to rapidly respond to change, whether it was technological or organizational. At one meeting about the new system development, the CFO of the company remarked that "we have just crossed the point from where technology supported our processes to where technology leads our processes."

Speed trumps efficiency

When innovation drives the market, getting there first is more lucrative than getting there cheapest. Extending the line from Schumpeter's business cycles and Christensen's disruptive innovation cycles we may well conclude that today innovation, through digital technology, happens in cycles that are so short and that have such great impact that organizations may no longer presume to achieve the so-called '*first-mover advantage*'.

Traditionally, theorists granted some advantage to the organization that was first to develop an innovative product or concept. The time required to copy such an innovation would give the original manufacturer the exclusive advantage to capture markets and build up customer loyalty before competition could step in. After this period, the market leaders develop efficiency and by the time competition steps up to the level of the first mover, the leader can produce at a much lower cost than market average.

Increasingly, though, rapid innovation cycles have rendered the time-to-copy (and even the time-to-improve) to almost zero, diminishing the time advantage. This does not mean, however, that first-mover advantage no longer exists. Experience has shown that first movers not so much enjoy a time benefit but a learning benefit.

Being first to launch means being first to learn from customer experience and hence being the first to be able to improve. Based on this idea, many organizations have adopted the principles of rapid iterative product development popularized by The Lean Startup (Ries, The lean startup: How today's entrepreneurs use continuous innovation to create radically successful businesses., 2011). The principles hinge around developing the smallest possible working product and testing it with real customers. Ries never intended this concept of 'Minimum Viable Product' (popularly named MVP) to solve the first-mover advantage problem; he intended to protect eager startups from wasting time and energy on over-developing a product without validating customer demand in the real world. But it turned out to be a very effective philosophy and strategy for creating a culture of rapid continuous development and continuous innovation.

Speed in continuous innovation can be achieved by relentlessly creating the smallest possible marketable product or improvement and bringing it to the market. This is best done by carefully capturing and analyzing feedback from the market through the collection of usage data—ideally with sensor data from the actual product. This feedback, together with the strategic product development road map, determines the next iteration of development. Especially in digital products and services, improvements may be marketed as quickly as a few weeks after the launch of the original MVP. But even in complex industrial development, such iterations can happen at a fast pace.

Car manufacturer Tesla Motors' entire production facility is operated as an iterative production process, with new model features being added to the production process as soon as they are available. Buyers do not purchase a particular model year version of the famous Model S, 3, X or Y. Instead, they purchase the version that is then available. It may well be that their version of the car is slightly more advanced or different in design from its predecessor or that it lacks a few sensors that the next customer may benefit from. Since each Tesla car is individually connected to the internet, software upgrades are performed automatically whenever they are ready for delivery, without intervention from the owner.

Some will now argue that, because the time benefit of first-mover advantage has been diminished, efficiency is now the key competitive advantage of being first, as it allows the first mover to drive costs down before others appear on the market. If all competitors are capable of delivering the same value, those who can deliver it cheapest will win, right? Wrong.

Achieving extreme efficiency comes at a high price in times of continuous innovation. Optimal efficiency requires a high degree of standardization and stability. Any changes to such a standard

– especially unexpected ones – drive up costs. As a result, designing efficiency requires reducing the number of options for change. Efficiency assumes that a product is best designed in a single iteration and then produced or operated stably over a continued period. Even though production and operational costs can be driven down in such a way, the opportunity to quickly adapt to market learnings diminishes greatly, and competitive advantage drains.

In the age of continuous innovation, efficiency quickly results in cheap products that are outdated compared to competitors. It is a downward spiral in which margins and longevity of the production cycle drop. Obviously, this is no argument to strop striving for cost reduction and operational common sense, but the opportunity for continuous innovation through fast and small iterations has changed the competitive landscape towards a world where efficiency has lost to speed in terms of strategic power.

It is by no means incidental that the trends of digitization and continuous innovation are closely followed by the trend of organizations to adopt the principles of Agile working. When digital technology and production methods allow organizations to adopt fast learning cycles and improvements, they require an organizational design that supports and even reinforces this speed. Agile teams, as I will show in chapter 14 | Agility matters, are often less efficient in strict terms of performance per individual. Yet they allow for far greater flexibility and speed and therefor result in a superior output in terms of customer value delivered.

Installed base trumps everything

All digital technology creates data. And when data is concerned, bigger *is* better. The value of data lies not in scarcity but in abundance. It lies in the ever-larger datasets as a basis for analysis, determination, and prediction. Large datasets are created by lots of transactions and interactions, performed by a large user group.

The members of such a group do not necessarily have to be customers, as long as they are consumers, and as long as they are loyal and numerous. After all, their behavior translates to analytical power that can be directed at transforming non-paying users to paying user or at creating valuable insights through a different business model. Where previously non-paying customers were mostly regarded as 'freeloaders' and profiteers, today they may well form the backbone of a valuable installed base of analytical power not paying with cash, but with data.

A large installed base of users reinforces the market position of its owners in impressive new ways. Testimony to this fact is Amazon's 'anticipatory shipping' patent, described in Chapter 8.6, for the preemptive shipment of products to clients to reduce delivery times. Praveen Kopalle, professor of marketing at Tuck School of Business at Dartmouth College, elaborates on this idea another step further in his article in Forbes.com, stating that analytics and predictions may even lead to the point where a product that has not actually been ordered may be delivered to households presuming that the recipient will be willing to pay for it, and in the ultimate case may even be offered for free, "...delivering the package to the given customer as a promotional gift may be used to build goodwill." (Kopalle, 2014).

Why would a giant like Amazon ship products without an explicit order from a customer? Because it can actually predict with a very high degree of certainty that they will be bought on arrival anyway. The loss incurred on return shipping (when the algorithm gets it wrong) or 'promotional gifts' (when the algorithm decides there may be a second chance) is likely to outweigh the market share gained on competitors by delivering without the actual purchase being made first. This market share is important, because it ensures a large dataset from which more detailed analysis is possible. Amazon's analytics work best on bigger datasets, and with bigger datasets, Amazon can get bigger.

The debate about the disruptive power of startups and lean tech companies for a long time hinged around the concept that young digital native organizations are quickly outpacing large incumbents because they are more flexible and adaptive to change. Yet increasingly it becomes clear that incumbents have one discerning advantage over startups: an installed base of products and services in an often-loyal customer base. Any effort that new digital contenders need to make to grow their user base is in direct competition with an incumbent that already services these customers with existing products and a powerful marketing and sales apparatus.

Large datasets trigger the same effect that is commonly known as 'the network effect': analytics on large datasets lead to better predictable business, more turnover, more data and thus an even larger dataset and an even more predictable business. Through careful design, this effect can be amplified further by applying the concept of 'reciprocity,' which I described in my previous book, The New Oil. Reciprocity is the principle by which data-driven products and services are designed in such a way that their use generates additional data, which is exclusive to the provider of the service.

For example, the availability of flights and hotel rooms around the world may be known to thousands of travel agencies. Any travel agent can resell hotel rooms through a website and charge a fee in commission for the sales lead. However, online broker Booking.com has collected extensive data about how its customers click and search its website, how long they stay on a page, where their mouse hovers and which preferences they have when finally booking. From this it builds personal profiles of likes and behaviors of individuals and enriches it through a range of services in its apps and e-mail traffic the company collects as much relevant data as possible about actual behavior both before and during their travel. In doing so, Booking.com has built an analytics database that is among the largest travel-related databases in the world.

This innovation has put Booking.com in a position where it will increasingly be able to offer instant matching results to the traveler's preferences and therefore increase its insights into travel behavior. Because it knows its prospective buyers and customers so well it is able to make personalized offers that outweigh competition. The analytical power not only helps Booking.com to build a better product, it often *is* the product. Booking.com's market power has become so strong that it no longer charges a referral fee to hotels for matching a traveler to a hotel, it requires hotel to place bids on the position of their offer on the search result pages at Booking.com. It will come as no surprise then than even the data about the bidding behavior of hotels is registered and analyzed to obtain the best possible return for Booking.com.

Ever since the 'dot-com bubble', entrepreneurs have frantically sought to create a large installed base. There has even been a time when most likely in the absence of viable online business models, 'attracting the most eyeballs' was synonymous for success and making money came second. Almost two decades later, we have learned that not being able to make sufficient money from a large group of clients is not a healthy business. However, we have also learned that making sufficient money from a small group of clients is equally limited. Competitive advantage starts with having the most data about most users. Not to make them pay, or even to make them pay more, but to make them pay your organization rather than someone else's in the market.

CHAPTER 10
Moving Through the
Plateaus

Knowing where you are is as important as
knowing where you want to go

I t is tempting to think that the roadmap to world domination in your market would be plotted to move through the three plateaus of the Innovation Strategy Matrix to success. Unfortunately, that is not the case. Innovation strategy is a means to an end, not the holy grail of corporate success (although it is a tantalizing thought, of course). If anything, it is a tool to help you locate where your organization is placed on the map, so that you may choose a sensible next destination.

There may be perfectly valid reasons for organizations to remain in Plateau 2 with a particular offering without ever intending to move to Plateau 3. Some organizations may offer services on Plateau 2 and Plateau 3 simultaneously, serving different audiences. For some organizations, Plateau 3 may never offer a viable business model at all. The three plateaus do serve a useful purpose though for organizations that want to achieve success in applying data-driven technology and business principles to their business, without falling into the pitfalls that come naturally with innovation and development.

First and foremost, the three plateaus serve as a reminder to you about where you are in data-driven development. As I've shown before, innovation strategy is as much about data and technology as it is about organization and processes that enable you to leverage the value of data. The first thing to consider when confronted with a plan or an idea to implement data-driven products, services, or business models is its position on the plateau model.

Innovation self-assessment Part II

Now, return to the drawing of the matrix you made earlier in this book. Now, with the understanding that you have, take your own organization's capabilities, resources, and activities as a starting point, and do the following for three innovations under development in your organization: ask yourself the following questions and mark the spot in the matrix where this innovation is:

1. Is the (data) technology needed for the plan familiar to your organization and within your organization's comfort zone to use or operate? Or is your organization very inexperienced with this kind of technology, its implementation or operation? Plot your position on the vertical axis, where the bottom of the axis represents the answer 'we are experienced and familiar with this technology' and the top of the axis represents 'we are highly uncertain about this technology.'

2. Is the market you are going to serve using this plan an existing customer base or a market that you already serve? Or is it a market you are not familiar with or for which you lack the right type of organization? Plot your position on the horizontal axis, where the left of the axis represents the answer 'we are familiar in this market and well organized and equipped to service it.' The right side of the axis represents 'we are highly uncertain about this market and not very well organized to service it.'

Be frank and place a dot on the intersection of the two axis-positions in the model. The position of the dot will provide insight into your next best actions and the potential pitfalls and opportunities. The table below shows the situations you need to consider when moving outside of the three plateaus.

Now, have a look at the model. Where do you think your organization should initiate more innovative activities? Which innovations could you think of that might fit that spot? Remember, innovations are not just technological, they can be business model innovations, innovations in packaging or logistics, They can be 'reverse innovations,' creating simpler or more low-tech versions of the product that you already sell… be creative, and most of all: don't do this exercise by yourself.

Gather a team of colleagues and spend two hours on it. You'll be surprised by the results. If you feel you have some interesting results, feel free to share them with me at arent@vantspijker.nl and you'll be sure to get a response!

The 'inefficiency zone' and the 'disruption zone'

The inefficiency zone

If your answers point to a position in the bottom left corner of the model, Plateau 1 or more up-and-right in Plateau 2, you are on the right track with innovation. However, you should make sure not to venture into the 'Inefficiency Zone.' In this zone, your organization runs the risk of investing too much in data and technology only to achieve finite efficiency improvements. More technology will not yield long term better results.

Why not? In Platform 1, you use more advanced technology and data solutions in your existing business, and you do not serve a new market or add substantial new value. If this is the case, your only aim to use the technology is to optimize efficiency. UPS uses advanced data analytics to determine the most efficient routes for its delivery vans, saving millions per year on time, fuel, and maintenance. Similarly, Verizon, one of the US's largest telecom providers, analyzes data to predict the cancellation of subscriptions – a phenomenon called 'churn' – in order to take positive action before the subscriber cancels.

The more advanced or unfamiliar the technology, the more expensive it is likely to be and the more impact it will have on your organization. For Verizon, adding more complex technology to combat churn will only be effective if every dollar invested in technology will yield more than one dollar in retained subscription fees. Simply adding more data or technology will ultimately not result in more efficiency. It is a dead-end.

The disruption zone

If your answers to the questions position your plan in Plateau 1 and you aim to use the data and technology to serve new markets, you may ask yourself why that has not happened before. After all, the opportunity must have been around for a while in the existing organization, since it had the capabilities and execution power before today. It is likely that, should you start to serve the new markets with your relatively 'low-tech' offering, you may come to realize that your new customers demand more advanced analytics or technological solutions. Since you operate and offer limited technological capabilities, you stand a good chance of being surpassed, or even disrupted, by competitors that offer these advanced solutions.

Ten to fifteen years ago, leading construction equipment manufacturers like Caterpillar and Volvo Construction Equipment started fitting sensors to their equipment to measure things like fuel consumption, tire pressure, and loads weight. These sensors monitored the vehicles' performance and initially alerted their drivers when something was wrong or depleted. Then, a few years ago, the companies started sending the sensor data from each individual vehicle to a platform where it could be monitored by fleet owners and site managers in real-time. The data started serving a second purpose.

This platform became a new product on its own,[2] serving a new type of customer and market. Construction Equipment now not only served a purpose as heavy-duty machinery to perform earthmoving tasks. The equipment data platform now offered site managers a means to track the efficiency of the site activity in real-time and better plan and manage construction progress.

Today, most equipment manufacturers offer a data platform to monitor data collected from a fleet of trucks. However, introducing a vehicle data platform at this point in time will no longer suffice to outperform competitors. Advances made by forerunners in the field are quickly causing 'datafication's gravitational pull' towards Plateau 2, which has an effect on all players. In April 2015, Caterpillar announced the formation of its Analytics & Innovation division, following the acquisition of analytics startup called Uptake. The move by Caterpillar raised the bar for all players in the market to develop serious data-driven offerings to at least a Plateau 2 level.

Caterpillar continues to challenge its competitors in this space, having started with advanced predictive maintenance in Plateau 1, via site management data platforms in Plateau 2 to the current development of integrated supply chain data management solutions. With its analytics platform *Cat Connect*, that already connects half a million vehicles, Caterpillar is clearly leading the industry by moving up and right in the model towards integral data-driven business models at Plateau 3. During a conference in 2017, Tom Bucklar, Director of IoT & Channel Solutions at

---

[2] My first book, *The New Oil*, refers to the case of Volvo CareTrack in more detail.

Caterpillar, mentioned that his company was not aiming to become a platform vendor or software company (Albertson, 2017). He was, however, very clear about the subscription-based business model for services that Caterpillar was developing. One particular company used Cat Connect to connect 16,000 pieces of equipment, only 3,000 of which were Caterpillar earth moving equipment. Such a customer will not only get integrated data and performance metrics to increase efficiency and performance, it will also feed Caterpillar integrated data about construction site dynamics that can be leveraged to all customers through subscription services. Just as Tom Bucklar put it "we're going to be a heavy equipment manufacturer, we sell big iron, that's what we do, but we're gonna leverage digital to help our customers be more successful."

The organizational change hurdle

It is tempting to think that the most valuable ideas in the matrix hide in the top right corner, waiting to be discovered and have their disruptive powers unleashed. Alas, in practice, there usually is no direct correlation between disruptive powers of an idea and value produced by an organization.

There is no single 'disruptive innovation' to conquer a market. No bucket of gold at the end of the innovation strategy matrix rainbow. The notion alone resembles the medieval quest for a single formula to turn lead into gold. Creating sustainable value from innovative technology requires inspiration, hard work, a great deal of common sense and most of all perseverance. The biggest obstacles are usually not in implementing technology, but in maintaining the organizational stamina and adaptability required to progress development through trying, testing, adapting and, when successful, trying the next idea.

As we have seen in the previous chapters, innovation strategy forces organizations to adapt to opportunities and market demand. It drives organizational change. Contrary to technology change, organizational change has a tendency to bounce back to its old shape. When new technology has been implemented in an organization to support and existing process, employees are either excited and happy or dissatisfied and vocal. But the decision to implement is never revoked. The architectural solidity of technology is firm; once technology has been implemented it quickly becomes connected to other systems and networks. Making adaptations is time-consuming and expensive changing back to the old is next to impossible.

Using digital technology and data to create innovative products and services brings with it new processes and potential new requirements for how to organize. As these products and services are not yet embedded in the existing organization they are regarded as a business opportunity, not an irrevocable decision. Embedding these innovations requires an organizational adaptation that in early stages is, strictly speaking, still optional—and that is exactly where the problems start. The bigger the change that employees in the organization have to deal with, the greater the risk of lack of support from them. Organizational change is hard enough when it changes the way in which the going concern is performed. Now imagine changing the way people work when the actual work they do also changes.

In Plateau 2, employees are often confronted with a fundamentally different way to deliver value to customers.

Remember the journalists from The Financial Times in the introduction of this book? Twenty years ago, they were asked to work with new technology to publish articles directly in the online version of the publication and to let go of the traditional deadline. The deadline, until then, had been the recurring culmination point of an often hectic 24-hour period of news and excitement. It was the highlight of the day and a moment of pride and purpose for journalists and editors.

Shifting focus away from the deadline for the print edition to the real-time publication of articles online was a mind shift in itself. However, it was not the only change that the people at the Financial Times were faced with. When readers started to understand that the actual news was not on the newspaper but on the site, the printed edition lost its timeliness. Especially in the business world of FT.com, time was of the essence, and the printed version quickly lost out to the online version in terms of value.

The introduction of technology had disrupted the status quo of news when it introduced a new variable in the equation: time. For the Financial Times, this new variable required a fundamental change in the way the company operated. For editors, it created a separation between publishing news and offering backgrounds and insights. For marketers, it offered myriad new advertising options, and for sales it meant a steady decrease in subscriptions to paper editions replaced by a difficult new business model. For IT, this change prompted a shift from a primarily supporting function to a mission-critical discipline.

FT.com could not make all of these changes overnight. However, it was under immediate threat from Yahoo. For a few years between 2001 and 2006, the organizational change between Plateau 1 and 3 seemed almost unbridgeable. The business model of Yahoo, in the top right corner of the model, turned out to be perpendicular to the business FT.com was organized for. Looking back on responses from other traditional publishers in similar circumstances and responses from many incumbents in different industries facing similar challenges reveals three possible strategies to choose from. In very generic terms, these strategies are:

Stick to Plateau 1 and move up

The goal in this strategy is to reinforce the existing strong points, focusing on proven value and the use of technology to increase efficiency and reduce costs. Effectively the strategy is to become the leanest player in the market and to beat incumbents at a pricing game from the very start.

While often effective at first, the new entrants will try to position themselves as playing in a different market. When successful, price advantages become less relevant and disruption of the incumbent markets becomes a fact. Eventually, incumbents will always lose in this strategy, as they do not develop technological or organizational skills to adapt to the newly formed market. The old market will inevitably shrink, leaving the incumbent with an increasingly difficult gap to bridge.

Jump to Plateau 3 and leverage size

In this strategy, incumbents use their installed base and financial resources to quickly develop a competing technology proposition. They try to gain a foothold while reducing the technology backlog to new entrants as quickly as possible. In essence, this strategy aims to use money as execution power to beat the competition at its own game.

Two scenarios are seen most often: the incumbent launches a well-funded separate entity as a competing startup, or the incumbent acquires the (disruptive) entrant to solve all problems in one move. The strategy has proven to be effective for many corporations throughout the world. The strategy does come with a specific downside: the incumbent itself does not really change. If the strategy does not include a plan for the phased change from Plateau 1 to 3, building on the knowledge and experience from the acquired entrant, the two entities might very well end up competing against each other anyway.

Iterative development through Plateau 1, 2 and 3

In this strategy, the incumbent decides to focus on gaining the necessary skills and experience to compete in future markets. The company embarks on a path of discovery from applying relatively simple technology in existing business solutions (Plateau 1) to offering increasingly more data-driven solutions in Plateau 2 and 3. The aim is not so much to reach a predetermined destination, but to gain as much knowledge and experience in Plateau 2 and 3 as possible. It seeks to discover, implement, learn, and adapt the organizational structure to continuously offer innovative solutions. While keeping rigorous attention on Plateau 1 performance and results, management of the company addresses issues and difficulties in innovative solutions by looking at the impact on future potential rather than on current performance metrics.

The goal of this strategy is not to defend or win a particular position, but to develop options for the future and to create an organization that is capable of adapting to change to leverage such opportunities. When executed convincingly and with enough vigor the strategy allows the incumbent to react to disruptive threats with targeted response and to seize opportunities without compromising existing operations. However, the strategy is costly in the sense that it forces the organization to direct a significant portion of its attention to things other than its core revenue-generating business. It is, by all means, a long-term strategy.

Developing a roadmap

It would be all too easy to think that the strategy of iterative development through the plateaus is the only successful strategy. It is not. Over the years, I have seen companies being effective in all of the three strategies mentioned. However, it is becoming clear that the first two strategies, no matter how effective, are in effect postponement of adaptation. Today's Plateau 3 technologies and disruptions will be tomorrow's operating standard, there simply is no stopping technology's progress. It is as if the background of the Innovation Strategy Matrix is in continuous motion from top right to bottom left. It slowly slides underneath the plateaus, changing Plateau 2 into Plateau 1, Plateau 3 into Plateau 2 with a new Plateau 3 emerging out of the future.

Markets and organizations will need to adapt, whether they like it or not. Postponement of action will build op pressure rather than solve a problem, let alone create a market opportunity. Over time, no other strategy than the evolutionary one is sustainable. It seems obvious that strategy A will retain profitability for some time, but that it eventually leaves the organization ill-prepared for change. Strategy B seems a better option, but this strategy too offers no guarantee that the organization of the incumbent will be able to deal with change. Even when losses are compensated through the ownership of the digital competitor, the parent company will eventually lose out.

Strategy C offers not so much a strategy to grow to Plateau 3, but a strategy to be able to keep pace with the market movement from top right to bottom left and go faster or slower at will. It is comparable to walking up a downward-moving escalator: if you walk at just the right pace, you will remain at the same position between two floors. Stop moving and you will be taken down, speed up and you will reach the next floor.

In essence, Strategy C is the execution of a process of moving to the next level based on learnings and experience. It would seem that the speed of development is dependent on the resources applied to this trial and error, and in a sense that is true. Yet the key to success lies not only in speed but for a large part in direction; in knowing where to try and learn.

In my consulting practice, I have learnt valuable lessons about the most effective way to execute iterative development. First and foremost, it is vital that you realize that your team is not chasing a single great innovative idea. In incumbent businesses, there is no such thing as 'the best plan,' 'the disruptive idea' or 'the next Uber'. The risk-averse organization simply will not have it.

There is, however, a mighty force that can be directed towards achieving astonishing results. Such direction starts by management creating a global vision for the (near) future in the area between plateau two and plateau three. Based on this vision, the organization collects existing ideas and generates new ideas for digital innovation and plots these ideas in each of the plateaus. Once plotted on the matrix, it becomes visible how each of the steps may be the stepping stone for the next idea. Perhaps because the technology developed in one idea form the basis of the technology required in another idea. Or perhaps because the clients for one idea may be the same as clients that were served with an earlier innovation. Or perhaps it may be as simple as a team gaining experience while working on one idea that is required to start working to realize a more complex innovation.

When the ideas and their interdependencies have been mapped, a roadmap can be drawn up from the bottom left of the matrix towards the management vision. Such a roadmap may consist of more than one path or even a split in tracks. Each time an idea has been realized, the roadmap should be re-evaluated and adjusted. Perhaps new ideas have surfaced, existing ideas may have been invalidated by experience. The roadmap helps to keep focus on achieving the management vision by reinforcing developments, starting in Plateau 1 and, building on newly achieved experience and insights, towards Plateau 2 and 3.

The roadmap becomes more effective when the ideas to be realized get smaller. Smaller ideas lead to a faster re-evaluation of the roadmap and more control over direction. Smaller ideas also limit the investment in time and money required for the realization. And smaller ideas lead to quicker and more certain victories. Chasing a gargantuan promise of innovative success leads not only to high expectations, these expectations are also built on a mountain of assumptions.

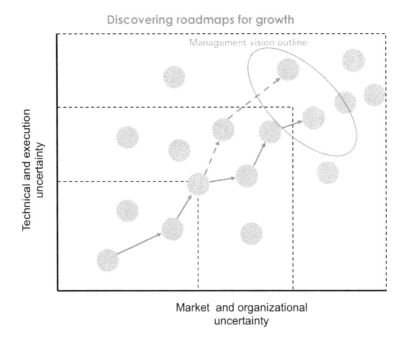

The goal of the roadmap is not to achieve the vision but to create the best possible first steps towards what today seems the best target. The journey is more valuable than the destination. The roadmap is covered with lessons that help to continuously reshape the vision. The most effective size for an idea on the roadmap is an idea that can be realized by a team of 5-7 enthusiastic people with relevant skills who spend 20% of their time (one day per week) on the realization of the idea for up to 12 weeks. Those 60 – 84 working days may seem very small indeed, but when following agile development methods such as Ries' *The Lean Startup* (Ries, The lean startup: How today's entrepreneurs use continuous innovation to create radically successful businesses., 2011) or Osterwalder's *Value Proposition Design* (Osterwalder, 2015) to guide the activities of the project participants, impressive results can be achieved.

In one example, one of my clients challenged a group of employees to spend one day per week, for six weeks, to create a dashboard that showed how much sustainable energy was being produced in real-time. The dashboard would use weather data and data about the location of solar panels and wind turbines that were available to the team. The challenge was met by performing a Six Weeks Innovation Challenge. Without any prior knowledge or understanding of the idea, the team of five people designed and developed the first dashboard and put it online within the designated six weeks.

Six weeks later the dashboard had been expanded and was presented to potential clients. They suggested adding weather prediction data to the algorithm so as to predict the amount of sustainable energy that would be produced on the next 14 days. For the clients, that insight proved to be very valuable in achieving their sustainability goals. In two additional six-week iterations, development proceeded; within six months of the team's first start, the dashboard was released to a paying client. The total cost was 120 person-days of work.

Start with a vision

Throughout this book, data, digital technology, and innovation have been continuously intertwined. It is easy to think that all things digital are 'innovative' and disruptive and that they require a 'eureka' moment to trigger. In practice, they do not. The roadmap through the plateaus usually does not start with a grand idea or innovation, but rather with a vision of what the market may look like in a few years' time, given the rate of development of digital technology.

Within that vision of the future market, management can formulate a position that it would want the company to be in that market at the given time. With that vision as a goal, the organization may develop its actions and transform both in terms of technology and organization. Such a management vision is pivotal in achieving results, specifically in large organizations. Digital technology and data are the raw material that forms any and all types of solutions. Ask a team the question which disruptive solutions it can develop based on the company's data and you are sure to hear solutions ranging from productivity apps to social networks to autonomous devices controlled by artificial intelligence.

Management vision helps to direct energy towards finding solutions that stay within the boundaries of the aspired market position. Why is that important? If we want to change the organization to adapt to the digital, data-driven future we must take one step at a time. We cannot demand the organization, which is still required to perform profitably in Plateau 1, to 'disrupt and pivot'. Hence, the first attempts to discover, learn and change should take place at a small scale within the boundaries of the known market: Plateau 1.

One step at a time

When I was first asked to discuss the problems of a big data project at the major newspaper publisher mentioned in Chapter 1, the company had already invested close to half a million Euro in setting up an advanced system of data collection and analysis with the aim to sell online personalized-ad services to advertisers. Even though in pilot setups the company was able to prove to advertisers that it could detect viewer preferences and serve matching ads on its websites, the company had great difficulty selling the new service to its major clients.

The technology may not have been flawless, but the project should have been able to attract the attention of a large customer base. It didn't. Customers did not buy. After months of trying, the board ordered to stop the project, feeling that this 'Big Data-thing' was a fad. Two of the project's brightest minds decided not to accept defeat and left the company, acquiring the technology from the publisher as they left to start their own business.

Within six months, the two workers returned to the publisher with an offer to buy bulk ad-space in the newspaper's website at slightly discounted prices under the condition that they could resell those spaces to their clients. The publisher's sales team regarded their former colleagues as new clients paying reasonable prices at high volume and struck an agreement. Within weeks, personalized ads started appearing in the empty slots, driven by the very same technology that the company had abandoned less than a year before. Although the sold ad-space was making good money for the publisher, a far larger chunk of margin was now flowing to its former employees' startup.

The problem, as it turned out, had not been in the clients not buying the personalized ads; it had been in the account managers not selling them. The sales team consisted of dedicated people who were fully tuned to selling single-ad placements directed at broad target groups for large corporate advertising campaigns. They had had great difficulty adapting to selling ad space that featured multiple ads directed at minuscule target groups in a continuous program. It was not the technology, not the market, not the business model, but organizational adoption that had failed.

The situation as described in the publisher's case is not unique. It resembles a pattern which is all too frequent in incumbent organizations. Change and innovation are often applauded and stimulated by an organization's leadership, but once they need to be embedded in the existing organization employees find it difficult to adapt and change. Contrary to popular belief, such difficulties mostly do not arise from employee's resistance to change. In my practice, I have come across far more people who are willing to innovate and change than across those who are not. Innovation is even considered a 'hot topic.' Failure to change is a system limitation. It is embedded in the design of the organization. It is caused by the organizational glass ceiling between Plateau 1 and 2.

It is important to have the organization start with a data-driven initiative that is below the glass ceiling. Remember that data is regarded by most people as a waste product of a process. It is almost exclusively used for reporting about what used to be, not for creating new value. If you ask people in any organization to use an unfamiliar tool to achieve a goal that is not their current responsibility, though they may respond enthusiastically, they will not likely use it.

However, if you show them how a simple version of such a tool and explain how it can contribute to the achievement of their current goals, they will put in time and effort and achieve positive results. This experience will achieve two things: acceptance of the tool as a positive contributor and a broader mindset as to what other, more advanced applications of such a tool might be.

To some, such an exercise may seem trivial. However, the objective of early-stage data-driven initiatives is not to immediately reap all of the benefits of the technology. It is to prepare and educate the organization on how to use new technologies to achieve the new management vision. How a company takes its first steps in embracing and developing innovations proves to be quite determinant for its future development.

The importance of the next best step

Realizing the first step in the data roadmap is as important as learning from it. The result is, however, far less important than the achievement itself and what it teaches us about the next steps. Obviously, the result is important: it is tangible value that has been created and delivered to the organization. But the risk of focusing on the result too much is that the organization will demand more short-term gains or improvements in the existing process. This is exactly what creates the glass ceiling.

The next step should be towards the vision in the direction of Plateau 2. The best way to guarantee such progress is to define explicit learnings at the end of the realization of each idea. These learnings should always cover three topics:

Technology learnings

What did we learn from this experience about technology and our capability to use and deploy it? What should we do differently next time? What should we try, keep, and avoid when developing the next idea?

Market learnings

What did we learn from our clients and our market-facing teams? Where do we see opportunities or threats in the market? Which customer demands did we experience? How can we learn from the user behavior we experienced? How can we use this to improve our next idea?

Organization learnings

How do we assess our own knowledge and expertise in this field? Where should we grow and who can we connect to in our own organization? How did we experience the support or resistance in our organization for our work? Which department or team would take responsibility for this idea if it were to be rolled out as a regular process or product? Do we feel they will be able to do so, and if not, what needs to change?

Choosing the next step in the roadmap is not simply a matter of looking at our earliest plan and following the lines. After each idea, we need to re-evaluate the roadmap based on the learning of the first iteration. Only then can we decide what the logical next step will be. Management involvement in this process is key to success. Management's vision should be broad and strategic enough not to be influenced by the experience of a single idea, but innovation should provide constant feedback to the organization, including to senior management.

Especially when choices need to be made between the development of two or more ideas, the learnings on market and organization become crucial. All people, including senior management, tend to base decisions on present-day experience and within 'the known universe' of the organization and market. Decisions about innovation will easily be misinterpreted as decisions about technology and the 'glass ceiling influence' becomes a reality. In innovation, we aim to break free from the present-day knowns. The learnings about the market and the organization help to communicate the broader context of the decision of what to develop next.

We shape our tools, then they shape us

In the long run, most of the value from data-driven innovations and business models come from products and applications that were not designed up-front, but that iterated towards their success. The development was achieved by teams that had learned step by step what technology could bring them and adjusted to the best results from these learnings.

However, the teams iterating their way towards a vision also tend to achieve results much slower than teams seeking to improve the existing line of business. Innovation teams appear to create little tangible value create while demanding real organizational changes. Teams working on incremental changes of existing products and services demonstrate concrete benefits within the existing way of working. These teams meet with far less pushback and resistance from managers and employees who, understandably, feel rather comfortable in improving with little difficulty. This presents a paradoxical situation in which short-term gain is sought after to overcome the system's resistance to change, while at the same time the focus should not be on the long-term development of innovative products and services.

This is why Continuous Innovation is an actual 'strategy' with an impact beyond the application of new technologies in an otherwise static environment. It is a new competence that, once acquired, allows for the adaption and improvement of the organization, market definitions, and business models. Rather than reinforcing the current business model through increased efficiency and margins, it enables changes that require the rethinking of operations and strategies.

Canadian scientist and media expert Marshall McLuhan best explained this situation in his famous quote "We become what we behold. We shape our tools and then our tools shape us."[3] The quote is important because it points out exactly how data-driven technology has an impact that reaches far beyond the initial impact of technology. Competitive advantage through data is not created by applying digital technology in the most effective way for the short term within the boundaries of today's corporation, but by organizations who are most capable to allow the tools to shape them into more competitive players.

---

[3] The quote is most likely not from McLuhan himself but from his good friend Father John Culkin, who made the quote when referring to McLuhan's work.

CHAPTER 11
Innovation's Omnipresence

The plateaus are in constant motion, moving down-left, with new plateaus emerging at the top-right

I f you asked a manager of a sizeable organization 25 years ago what he thought were his company's most valuable assets, the answer probably would have been 'people' or 'knowledge'. Ask the same question today and the more likely answer to get is 'data.' Both answers are somewhat amusing since neither people nor data are actually considered 'assets' by the organization, in the sense that they do not appear as a value on the balance sheet.

The answer that 'data' is considered the most valuable asset is even more interesting if you consider that Fortune 500 companies are among the most asset-laden organizations in the world, yet the data-driven business models thrive when combined with a massively decentralized asset base, such as the privately-owned 'taxis' in the case of Uber and real-estate in the case of AirBnB. Obviously, not all industries are very prone to this type of decentralization. As mentioned before, commercial airlines will not have to fear competing fleets of privately-owned Boeing 747s. Neither will gas stations need to fear the rise of home-grown biofuel outlets, although there is a very good reason to fear home-grown 'electricity stations' for charging electric cars, that will render traditional gas stations obsolete.

Technological advances that rely on the principles of datafication rapidly find applications in the decentralization of assets. Low-cost windmills and solar panels, owned and operated by private individuals, form a huge network of energy providers that are directly competing with commercial utilities via digital communities.

Similarly, 3D printers owned by enthusiasts and small firms are now commercialized through 3D Hubs, a company that takes orders for printing 3D objects and outsources the printing part to well over 22,000 3D printer owners all over the world.

The Weather Company, a commercial venture from Atlanta Georgia, uses a network of over 100,000 connected weather stations, operated by amateur meteorologists around the world, to better predict the weather around the globe. The 40,000 decentralized weather stations in its network in the US stand in stark contrast with the 3,500 stations owned by the U.S. National Weather Service.

Many examples of similar outsourcing-made-possible-by-digital-technology options can be found in helpdesk services, analytics, computing power, and design. Such digital innovations actually stand as testimony to Clayton Christensen theory of 'disruptive innovation'. Christensen points out that disruptive innovations tend to start with an offering that is perceived by the market as 'inferior' or aimed at low-end segments of the market. These offerings then move up-market serving mainstream customers while preserving the advantages that drove their early success.

When solar panels first arrived on the market, utilities did not see a viable consumer market and left the deployment and utilization of expensive photovoltaic panels to niche players and private individuals. After years of neglecting this niche market, the operational production capacity of energy through solar panels has soared and new energy-data marketplaces allow solar panel owners to trade their surplus energy with each other, without the mediation of utilities. This catapulted solar energy to the mainstream market, bypassing traditional asset-based energy producers who are now competing against a vast network of decentralized assets.

25 years ago, technological innovation created an advantage for the organizations who were first to develop the technology and turn it into a profit-generating asset. In those days, competitive advantage was in barriers to entry created through asset ownership. Today, ubiquitous digital innovation creates an advantage for organizations that are capable of continuously recognizing and leverage the opportunities created by the

technology without relying on asset-driven barriers to entry. Competitive advantage is in adaptiveness and agility. In that context, a 150-year old quote attributed to Charles Darwin[4] is now truer than ever in the corporate world: "It is not the strongest of the species that survives, nor the most intelligent. It is the one that is most adaptable to change."

Two identifiable changes

The adaptation to digital technology and data – *datafication* – is different for each individual company. Its impact depends on the company's vision for the future, its technological and execution capability, the markets it serves, and the organizational structure it operates. But there is one thing that makes datafication equally important for all organizations. Datafication impacts the market in a broader sense by triggering two identifiable market dynamics that are relevant to essentially every corporation:

1. Datafication pushes economic value forward in the value chain
2. Datafication pushes innovation down into the market

---

[4] In The New Oil, I explain that Darwin never actually used the phrase. It was falsely credited to him by Leon C. Megginson, professor in marketing at Louisiana State University, in 1963.

Datafication pushes economic value forward

Although popular opinion has it that traditional assets have become obsolete with the advent of datafication, nothing could be more besides the truth. The belief was popularized in the quote Tom Goodwin, Senior Vice President of Strategy and Innovation at Havas Media, when he stated that, "Uber, the world's largest taxi company, owns no vehicles. Facebook, the world's most popular media owner, creates no content. Alibaba, the most valuable retailer, has no inventory. And Airbnb, the world's largest accommodation provider, owns no real estate."

Goodwin wrote this paragraph as the start of an article on TechCrunch.com about how 'the battle is for the customer interface' (Goodwin, 2015). He explains how "…these companies are indescribably thin layers that sit on top of vast supply systems (where the costs are) and interface with a huge number of people (where the money is). There is no better business to be in."

Goodwin is correct about how data is quickly becoming the dominant connector between supply (products) and demand (customers). However, his quote has become popular for another reason. All of the companies he mentions in his example seem to be replacing the supply of 'products' from a small number of professional asset providers to a system of distributed supply, mostly from SMB's (Alibaba), individual entrepreneurs (Uber) and even private individuals (Facebook and AirBnB). Popular business wisdom frames this as if the digital 'layer' could outpace the corporate asset's economic value and render asset-centric businesses obsolete.

Apart from the fact that this is not what Goodwin intended, it is also not true. It is not very likely that we'll see initiatives such as Uber replace the airline industry by matching holiday travelers with private owners of aircraft. Nor will individuals be selling gasoline or packaged milk out of their homes anytime soon, no matter how slick the app may be. There simply is a need for production and operation of goods, such as commercial airliners, car fuel, and fast-moving consumer goods. This production most often requires capital-intensive assets.

Goodwin's point is that corporations need to change the way they look at the economic value of their asset base; ownership and centralized management of assets is not necessarily a competitive advantage anymore. Markets will no longer be very willing to pay a premium for the organizational capacity of corporations to own and operate centralized assets. Whether competing decentralized options are available or only centralized options exist, economic value is created increasingly by data and seldom by assets.

On hindsight, it is interesting to see how industries such as personal transport (and indeed even parcels or home delivery), hotels, retail, and publishing have long relied on the exclusivity of access to enough assets to build a profitable business. That era has now passed and corporations in every industry need to reconsider the origin of their competitive powers.

Data outpaces the economic value of assets in more than one way. Firstly, as explained before, asset ownership brings fixed costs that need to be amortized over a fixed period. Competing propositions relying on decentralized assets can calculate costs relative to the scale of production and are therefore cheaper. Even though this principle is in no way new and existed long before 'datafication', the datafication trend effectively separates propositions in data-driven services and assets-driven 'production.'

Secondly, data shifts corporate emphasis from the optimal utilization of assets to the optimal provisioning of service. After all, if nobody owns all of the assets, optimal customer service can never interfere with maximum efficiency. Of course, in the data-driven version, the cost of inefficiency is spread over each individual asset provider. Decentralized assets offer quicker innovation because asset amortization is placed at somebody else's account: this leads to less efficiency in asset utilization across the market, but with smaller impact on the system as a whole and with greater customer focus.

Because assets are required to fulfill customer needs, they are still important in the value chain. However, assets ownership used to mean (and in many cases still means) having an exclusive capability to perform a task and make margin. One had to own the hotel room to operate it and to make the profit. One had to own the taxis to drive them and make the profit.

Increased economic value

It is often said that digital disruptors such as Uber and AirBnB gain most of their margin by decentralizing their assets to private individuals. This is not necessarily the case. In most economic theories, the decentralization of assets would lead to greater inefficiency in the market. The theories presume that economic gain, or margin, is to be obtained by companies centralizing these assets and optimizing their utilization, thereby reducing the cost per unit produced. The optimization comes at a cost though, such as in centrally housing the assets, logistics, capital investment, and risk. In data-driven business models focusing on decentralization of assets, such as those of Uber and AirBnB, this economic theory still stands, for these companies do not solve the optimization problem through ownership and central management of the assets, but through the use of data, algorithms, and apps. The costs for housing, logistics and capital investments and risk are much lower for AirBnB but they are likely higher for the owners of the decentralized assets. For the digital disruptors, the management of decentralized assets comes at an additional cost compared to centralized providers. Costs such as for platform management, app development and operation. The competitive edge of these business models lies in the decentralization of ownership (and risk) of assets because private asset owners tend to calculate a lower depreciation of their assets and usually calculate no risk fees or interest on capital investment. Yet from the client perspective, costs are usually no driver to choose the competitor. In most cases, the reason to choose a decentralized competitor lies in its additional customer value compared to centralized asset-based business models. Benefits a centralized provider simply cannot match: the scale of the fleet at Uber, the number of rooms available at AirBnB, the number of editors on Facebook.... Digital technology and data have shifted focus away from the ownership of assets to the availability of production capacity.

In the era of digitization, value shifted forward in the value chain. Digitization of the booking systems initially reduced booking costs for the hotel owners. When hotels allowed third party booking companies to offer what were then regarded as 'online travel agents,' initially these companies brought more traffic to the hotels and offered more value to the customer, such easy selection of alternatives. In the process, value started shifting forward in the value chain, from the property owners to the data owners. With datafication, control over the flow of data in the booking process allowed third parties to marginalize the value of assets in favor of ownership of customer knowledge. Today the system that was initially regarded by property owners as beneficial because it brought in more traffic now backfires on them and draws economic value away from hotels.

Data-driven business opportunities force the unbundling of asset-based offerings and customer service. If asset owners are locked in a business model in which asset management is a prerequisite for service provisioning, then they are highly likely to be disrupted. They will fall prey to data-driven parties that can leverage profit without the need for owned asset management, such as Uber and AirBnB.

It would be easy to say that asset owners are in the wrong place and are fighting a lost cause. They are not. It is, however, relatively easy for asset owners to become trapped in a space where asset management and service provisioning are inextricably linked to make a profit. These systems are extremely vulnerable to disruption, so asset owners must find new ways to make money from their owned assets.

The value of an organization is not determined by the value of the assets on its balance sheet, but by the way in which it can generate free cash flow from those assets. If the company, through competition from data-driven players, is no longer able to generate this cash flow from the services it provides on top of the assets it should build an unbundled business model consisting of two separate parts. One that is based on leveraging the original asset at low margin to its maximum capacity, without a service markup and with the aim to generate as much data as possible. And another that is based on leveraging the data that its assets generate and that is required by data-driven parties to market their services.

Services are always at the front of the value chain

Over the last ten years, customers value has shifted from what is generally viewed as the core product (a car, a computer, a newspaper, electrical power) to the services accompany the product, such as the connectivity to a smartphone, the news notifications, and the smart meter. Tesla Motors set a new standard when it introduced automatic software updates in the Model S luxury sedan. Renowned newspapers such as the Financial Times and Wall Street Journal are valued for the quality of their apps and alerts as much as for their content. Utilities are expected to offer insights and energy savings tips to consumers even if that means that they will sell less energy.

Services are always in front of the value chain. Anything that stands between the customer and the data-driven service is often considered waste by the customer. Services empower the consumer, make it easy for consumers to interact with the brand, use the product and share the experience with others. Although the product is the basis for all value, without services, the product decreases in value significantly. That is why data-driven services are increasingly valuable in the value chain.

Despite this, many organizational business models are still centered around the production and management of the physical product. A case made clear when Nest Labs, a Silicon Valley tech-startup that produced a rather neat looking digital home thermostat was acquired by Google. The company was founded by former Apple engineers Tony Fadell and Matt Rogers in 2010 and was bought by Google four years later for US$3.2 billion. Few people at Honeywell, one of the world's largest manufacturers of thermostats, would have regarded Nest a threat to their business in early 2014, let alone value the 280-employee strong company at more than 10% of the market capitalization of the 130,000-employee corporate behemoth. If anything, Honeywell executives may have frowned (or even smiled) at Nests modernistic design variation of the iconic Honeywell circular home thermostat. But at Nest, the thermostat is not regarded as the product. It is regarded as one of the user interfaces for its broad service in energy purchase, supply, usage, and savings.

The Nest thermostat digitizes the entire temperature-control process in a home. It is permanently connected to the internet, measures real-time energy consumption by heating and appliances, such as washing machines and air conditioning, and forecasts energy consumption. It then reaches out to utilities, helping them to optimize production and generate efficiency savings. It does so by manipulating energy consumption in individual homes and saving money for consumers by turning down the air conditioning a few degrees when prices are high due to peak usage.

Nest generates business value in a number of ways. The first is through its 'far higher than average price for a thermostat.' Nest retails at close to three times the price of, let's say, a Honeywell thermostat. But consumers do not regard that a sound comparison. After all, with Nest, they are not purchasing a thermostat but an energy service.

The second way in which Nest creates value is through its interactions with utilities. The optimizations in efficiency that Nest provides to utilities is not donated to them for free. They pay a percentage of their savings to Nest. And thirdly, a piece of the savings made by consumers is also reverted to Nest. So, unlike a traditional thermostat manufacturer like Honeywell (which in the meantime has adopted Nest's 'connected' features in its own offerings) Nest is not only playing the US$3 billion global market for thermostat hardware, it is actively playing a role in the US$6 trillion global market for energy.

Data drives focus on customer experience

In The New Oil, I dedicated a chapter specifically to what I called the principle of 'reciprocity': the activation of a mechanism in a data-driven model that ensures the flow of usage data from a product or service back into the company. Reciprocity is important because it creates an uncopiable advantage. No other company can create the same data from the usage of your product through your systems.

Usage data can be as simple as a sensor detecting a single action, as in counting the number of times a door was opened, or the number of people walking by a store. Data can also be a bit more complex, as in the measurement of a sequence of activities, like the number of people walking by a store combined with the number of times the shop door was opened and the number of purchases that were made in the same period. This last sequence can tell us something about how many people that walk by a store actually enter the store and make a purchase. This chain of actions can be seen as a pattern. Analytics technology can sift through the data from all sensors, detect such patterns and, based on historical data, can predict what will happen next in each stage of the pattern.

Typically, in Plateau 1, data adds value when this type pattern analytics helps to predict and automate known processes, such as the maintenance of a car: sensors detect vibrations in a wheel, analyze this data and conclude that in 81% of all known cases, these vibrations are a precursor to damage in the car's suspension. This causes the system to automatically schedule a maintenance appointment at the garage nearest the location where the car is parked most often during night times.

As a rule of thumb, the more complex the pattern, the more valuable the potential business cases. Data-driven solutions in Plateau 1 are often limited to the organization's existing processes because the patterns they serve are reasonably predictable and understandable. When we introduce more complexity into the pattern, such as new datasets or more direct usage feedback, the pattern can result in more outcomes which can form previously impossible business cases.

For example, when we allow a car access to the driver's calendar app and to the business hours of nearby auto shops, its system could detect a failing suspension and plan a repair stop at the nearest garage along the itinerary of the driver when they have time available to stop for repairs.

This kind of data-driven service lies beyond Plateau 1. Still, the idea of planning time in calendars to repair a car is predictable. The data itself still is not very variable, there is just a lot of it. The reason for this is that systems tend to perform rather simple tasks: the wheel spins, the garage operates a work schedule, and a calendar reminds us of our planning. Value could increase even further if the data collected has no particular predictable nature.

As such, we focus not on the systems and their connected activity, but on their users and everything they do, everything changes. Tracking people rather than devices creates an endless stream of data from the devices that they use in the order and in the location in which they use them. If we are in some way able to determine *who* controls a device, we open up a galaxy of possibilities. For now, we can combine sensor data from the car with previous driving behavior of the driver, his location behavior through his phone and his previous attendance at meetings to offer the following service. The car will notice the suspension failure and alert the driver that his driving behavior is causing technical damages to the car. It will measure if the driver responds by driving more carefully and for how long. The insurance company may have the car repeat the warning in due time or charge extra for reckless driving.

The system will then validate each of the meetings in the driver's calendar for importance: the upcoming appointment in the calendar was rescheduled from last month to today, canceling that one for a quick repair is probably not possible. The next appointment recurs every week so that is the likely candidate to skip, but GPS from the driver's phone indicates that the driver was somewhere else last week and skipping twice in a row is not advisable. The third upcoming meeting is labeled 'Quick update with Mike on project X.' What if the quick update could be done by phone or at the garage? The system can send a calendar request to the driver to change the location of the meeting to 'Call' or 'At garage' and then plan the appropriate garage appointment.

The example above is fictitious but not impossible. Current developments in artificial intelligence make this a realistic possibility rather than a future prediction. It is also an indication that when personal behavior data is involved possibilities become virtually endless. Much value can be created by collecting usage data from individual people and their use of devices or services.

Sensor data from single devices is generally used to achieve Plateau 1 benefits: efficiency and speed. It requires no specific organizational change or market strategy. When complexity increases and sensor data is combined with other sensory technology and external data, more complex, Plateau 2 offerings become possible that impact the processes and potentially the market proposition. When a few years ago BMW introduced predictive maintenance on all cars, it caused more than a stir with brand dealers who earned most of their living on maintenance. Much of that revenue now disappeared because cars were sent to be fixed before the damage occurred rather than after.

Most new Plateau 2 and 3 value is derived from the creation of individual user profiles. With it, naturally, comes great responsibility and vigilance for an individual's privacy, but that is not the key point here. The usage data is important because it allows building a profile of the user and his/her individual use of the service. Based on this insight you may then adapt your service to this usage.

A good example is the Nest thermostat, which will automatically adjust your room temperature based on your previous settings of the temperature dial. After a few weeks, Nest will have deducted from your actions how and when you like your room to be heated and then change the temperature automatically. Or perhaps you have noticed that on your smartphone Google will remind you that the journey you are about to undertake will last slightly longer than it normally does because of congestion. Google has measured your travel behavior over time and calculated when you are most likely leaving and where you are likely going.

Usage data from individual people allows for the most valuable services. Services become the key differentiator in competition because personal feedback data is unique to each supplier. Users will continue to use the service as it becomes highly personalized. That usage generates more data, which in turn is used to provide the service.

This does lead to a delicate balance in which user data becomes the driving force behind a service. Once Amazon's recommendations become poor, the online giant will little more than a storefront like many others, once Nest starts turning the heat up when you are not in, or turn it off when you are, the service is worthless. When you stop using it, less data flow to it, and the service becomes even worse.

Customer experience, then, becomes a critically important part of collecting usage data. A smart customer experience leads not only to better data collection, but also to more. Companies like Facebook, Booking.com and Amazon are experts at trying out new interfaces, new clickable options to discover customer responses to ideas, and do so at a rate of sometimes hundreds of tests per day. Less all-online, but equally aimed at gathering usage data are car manufacturers using apps to let drivers collect usage data, retailers offering loyalty cards to register purchases and even employers using employee security passes and account data to measure employee satisfaction.

Using behavioral data to squeeze as much money as possible out of your customer through cross- and upselling is not a long-term strategy. Remaining in Plateau 1 in this way will eventually hollow out your organization's competitive position. The importance of the customer experience is two-fold: first of all, data allows you to tailor the customer experience to the specifics needs and wishes of each individual customer. Furthermore, the customer experience should be developed in such a way that it collects more data about customer behavior. At some point it should become unclear whether you offer a particular product because your business model is to sell a great product at a profitable margin or if you are offering that product in order to collect data to optimize multiple other propositions.

For Spotify, the 'playlist' feature does not only serve as a great way for users to organize their favorite songs. Playlists also create insights into which music goes together well for people. If out of the millions of playlists a few thousand playlists feature both the song 'Beat it' by Michael Jackson and the song 'What goes around comes around' by Justin Timberlake appear, then Spotify could offer the Timberlake song as a suggestion to new playlist creators that just added 'Beat it' to their list. From the perspective of Spotify, the playlist is both a feature to sell to subscribers and an advanced data collection tool. The customer experience of the playlist is the double-edged sword where customer value is delivered and data for future value is being harvested.

Datafication pushes innovation down into the market

Already in the late 1990s, in the ramp-up to the dot-com bubble, digital technology startups proved their disruptive force on incumbent businesses. With no legacy systems, labor force, customer contracts, or financial obligations, these often well-financed nothing-to-lose endeavors could take maximum risk at trying out radical new approaches, inventing technological breakthroughs along the way.

Of course, we must take into account the tremendous cost at which this disruptive market renewal takes place. During the "dot com bubble" and to this day hundreds of innovative startups fail for everyone that creates a profitable business. Venture

Capital research firm CB Insights calculated in 2014 that over the previous five years failed startups in Silicon Valley, on average, raised US$1.3 million before going bust (CB Insights Inc., 2014). The 2016 study on startups, performed by Startup Genome, concluded that well over 90% of startups fail (Startup Genome, 2016).

With those numbers, it is safe to assume that for each successful disruptive business investment of well over US$100m is made in capital sacrifices. It would be too simple to disregard that investment as 'waste.' Although the investment did not return any value to its shareholders or investors, the bankrupted tech companies often leave a technology legacy that others learn from or even build upon.

The value of startups lies not in aggregated assets, processes, and market share, but in ideas, concepts, failures, and learnings. Each of which is easily (and often quite intelligently) copied from a failed startup to next potential market disruptor. Remember that the startup scene thrives on meetups, network events, hackathons, collaboration, and a healthy drive to outperform the next team in terms of bright ideas and technical brilliance.

Even when its products' inner workings are kept extremely secret, every startup will influence its peer group with fresh ideas, solutions, and business models. The startups that do make it to the scale-up phase often have been greatly influenced by the ideas and experiences of their late peers. Even though each technology startup acts as a single entity and investors place their bets on individual ideas and teams, the combined investment in the digital technology ecosystem works as a single innovative force in the marketplace.

This force creates an almost continuous flow of new solutions and business models into the market, creating a new status quo in which these innovative business models are norm. Consumers (both in B2B as in B2C markets) are treated to an array of innovative solutions, some of which fail quickly, some stay the course, and some of which define new market standards. The combined impact of each of these solutions creates an awareness of and demand for new technological solutions, product categories and business models.

From the perspective of incumbents, the market has moved from the top right in Innovation Strategy Matrix to the center position of 'New processes in existing business.' Without any action from their side, incumbents have become old fashioned. Not because they were outpaced by existing rivals or a single startup, but because the market has moved to a different norm. It is important to realize that the new norm has not been set from the perspective of technology but from the perspective of the new business models that were enabled by technology.

Over the last decade, one of the most profound changes in the business landscape is the 'contagiousness of data-driven business models.' When new innovative business models catch on, they become the new norm at lightning speed. How many times have you heard companies label themselves as 'the Uber of X' or the 'AirBnB of Y'? In data-driven innovation, technology and business go hand-in-hand.

Innovative new business models over time become the new market standards, which become business as usual. Plateau 3 becomes Plateau 2, then Plateau 2 becomes Plateau 1. Technological developments change markets and their business models. When markets and business models change, organizations that remain motionless fall behind. However, opportunity lurks for incumbent organizations that can move against the business model's motion from Plateau 3 to Plateau 2 quickly and without losing touch with its markets. These organizations create compelling competitive advantages in their ability to scale and adopt new technology in existing marketing and production operations. They can outperform technology startups that face the problem of scaling-up both their market reach *and* their organization as their products become mainstream.

Compared to most startups, incumbents can bring to bear an impressive array of resources to effectively counter or absorb the disruption that startups are trying to achieve. Financial resources, a large sales force, development resources, and the ability to quickly mobilize a sizable and actionable organization - often larger than the startups that are directly threatening them.

Although startups lack the resources that incumbents can muster, they are usually free to focus all on one goal. Incumbents need to balance their concerns between the running operation and a disruptive threat that by many in the organization will be regarded as fad or hype. Even when the threat is taken seriously, the incumbent still needs to focus its resources in the right direction, towards Plateau 2. The natural response against market threats in an organization is to adopt the competing technology to improve or expand the existing offering. The organization would grow from Plateau 1 upwards into the inefficiency zone (see page 155) or horizontally into the disruption zone (see page 156).

As I will show later in part three of this book, the new core competence of any incumbent will be to balance resources between the running operation and the new digital capabilities, and to continuously rebalance and refocus efforts to achieve the best growth opportunities.

Competition starts between Plateau 2 and Plateau 3

Competitive positioning in data-driven disruptive technology starts in Plateau 3. Even though in most cases it is not recognized by most players. Innovative solutions developed by many different actors are being introduced into the very corners of the market and either fail or slowly edge away at the existing business. Neither the startups nor the incumbents have a full understanding of the shift that is slowly starting to take place. Only when one or two initiatives begin to gain traction and convert larger groups of customers to the new solutions will the market respond in unison: startups will copy or transform to proven offerings and business models and incumbents will regard the united adoption of a new 'standard' as a first sign of a future threat. In essence, the market shifts downwards from Plateau 3 to Plateau 2.

It is in this area, somewhere between Plateau 3 and Plateau 2, that management in most incumbent firms will seriously consider the threat of disruption and/or the opportunities of the new market options. And even here, they will have to work hard to convince many of their own colleagues of the threats and opportunities. The new market models are thin at best, unproven and often dependent on the positive outcome of many assumptions: 'if many people adopt the technology…,' 'if sensors become cheap enough…,' 'if the market will continue to ….'

For managers, competing against Plateau 3 innovations is like fighting a ghost. It's usually quite easy to sum up a number of arguments why *not* jumping the bandwagon is actually a sane decision. The thoughts and arguments resonate through their heads: "We've asked our customers about it and they don't want it." "Why don't we let these startups figure out the hard part and then buy them *and* their clients?" "I can see it working for some niche markets, but we should focus on providing real value to our real customers."

This is the epitome of the classic evasive discussion that Christensen described in his article "What is disruptive innovation?" The sensible thing to do for incumbents is to wait and see and focus on high priority clients. And exactly there is where the disruption takes place: disruptive technologies develop in niche markets and having gained traction there quickly spread to mature markets. Incumbents are left incapable of closing the gap fast enough because existing clients still need full attention. The disruption not only comes from a change in technology but from a change in business model.

Plateau P+1

For incumbents, competition in the Innovation Strategy Matrix usually starts when disruptors move down from Plateau 3 to Plateau 2. In doing so, they enter the market space in which incumbents see growth and feel comfortable. Although the competition is not immediately threatening the core business of the incumbents, incumbents will regard the move as a threat to future potential. That is why this competition is not about getting the most revenue, but about getting the most knowledge and experience. There is, after all, no procurable substitute for experience.

In the late 20th century, when Clayton Christensen described his theory on disruptive innovation, the landscape he portrayed was that of a smaller competitor undercutting the market of incumbents by targeting seemingly uninteresting niche markets. His advice to readers was to discover such players in their own or adjacent markets and formulate a response by either adapting existing products to meet the inferior offerings of the new entrants or create new operating companies to compete with the new entrants.

Less than 20 years later, incumbents no longer have the luxury of time to discover threats and formulate a response. Instead, ongoing technological development around the globe has brought innovative disruptive power to virtually any organization. It would be futile for incumbents to assume that they have time to search for and discover Plateau 3 competitors and formulate a response from their threats.

In reality, every organization faces a steady stream of Plateau 3 innovations moving down to Plateau 2 and threatening the growth markets and even the Plateau 1 core markets of incumbents. And every time that such a move takes place, the Plateau 3 technologies become more maturely developed, more widespread and adopted into a broader context. A good example of such developments is in the Internet of Things. By 2010 sensor technology was only slowly making its way into the agricultural sector, with key players like John Deere and Lely, leading innovators in their field, regularly being challenged by small startup companies developing add Ad-on products or even competing alternatives to their offerings. The traditional response of the incumbents was to take time, analyze market developments and, when the time seemed right, to acquire the incumbent and its technology.

Today, competing digital innovations continuously find their way into the incumbent's markets. So many in fact that the traditional approach to 'spot-analyze-acquire' strategy is no longer effective. Digital technology has become the norm in the agricultural sector. Farmers operate their business from their offices almost as often as from their machines: cows are milked by milking robots, self-driving tractors plow the fields, and irrigation systems adjust the fertilization of the land-based on the hourly weather forecast.

Many of these technologies were not invented for the agricultural sector but were adopted from other business so quickly that incumbents had no time to formulate a response. Both John Deere and Lely, innovators at heart, have responded swiftly by recognizing the importance and speed of digital technology and now own extensive digital development centers in which they develop their own digital innovations with same vigor and dedication as Silicon Valley startups (and for good reason).

Developments move so fast and adoption of technology is so relentless that plateau three innovations continuously mature and move down to Plateau 2, and from Plateau 2 to Plateau 1. For incumbent organizations, this development is best compared to walking up an escalator: even to remain in place in the market the organization needs to innovate at a constant pace.

To reach Plateau 3, the organization not only will need to innovate, but it will also need to innovate faster than its rivals. There is an upside for incumbents though: where startups have the luxury of being able to start at Plateau 3, with no legacy and no commitments, incumbents have the luxury to use their wealth to buy into the developments of Plateau 3. Their innovative power lies in creating and maintaining partnerships with the digital fearless and in scaling and embedding their innovations into the incumbent organization. Mind you, this is different from the traditional acquisition strategy. Incumbents no longer have the time to scan the market for acquisition candidates in Plateau 3. Yet they are an attractive partner for the digital fearless to continuously work together on the rapid development of applications based on Plateau 3 technology and thus to combine the strengths of both organizations. In the age of continuous innovation, however, the key strength of the incumbent here is not the capital to acquire the desired technology, but the agility to team up with new, small partners to integrate their innovations into the organization.

Trending uncertainty

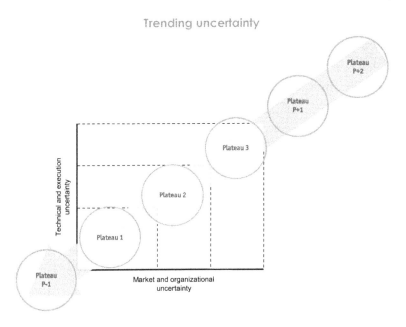

For Plateau 2 innovations, the required organizational capability is more structural than the aforementioned plateau and expertise to adopt the most viable Plateau 3 options for future growth and embed them into the running business. By design, incumbents tend to assimilate any outside initiative into the existing structure of the organization: its hierarchy, processes, standards, and architecture. This urge actually makes sense; remember that the incumbent is designed to minimize risk and generate a maximal return on investment in assets.

In the era of continuous innovation, assimilation of innovations is counterproductive. It does not create more value in the future from standardization to scale, it creates less value because it uses existing resources to reduce the future potential of the innovation. In Plateau 2, the incumbent should actively work to adapt the organization to fit the requirements of the innovations rather than the other way around. This poses a somewhat strange problem to management, however. It is in management's best interest to keep the organization as stable as possible to reduce risk and maximize profit from a standardized process. On the other hand, though, the stable organization will need to change to accommodate rapid consecutive market developments. How does one merge the stability required for a profitable business with the adaptability required to leverage innovative developments?

The answer to this question starts with the understanding that in Plateau 1, the organizational structure should not be optimized to accommodate the current market and offerings, or even a hypothetical future market, but instead a continuously changing market. If Plateau 2 and 3 developments move down into the 'regular' market at a constant pace, a rigid Plateau 1 organizational structure will very much resemble the ground level in the escalator metaphor I used earlier; when you stop walking up a downward escalator you will move backward with you back turned towards the ground. Stand still long enough and you will reach the ground floor unexpected, and the continuing downward-moving steps will tip you over.

Continuous Innovation is as much about organizational design as it is about technology. In the following chapters, I will explain how successful organizations use adaptive organizational design and a predictable process to accommodate innovation while maintaining the stability and effectiveness to retain the current competitive advantage.

PART III
Creating Continuity

CHAPTER 12
Balancing Concerns

Today, organizations need both stability and
adaptability to change

Between 2010 and 2016, Volvo Cars, the Swedish car manufacturer renowned for its relentless focus on safety, was the subject of one of the world's longest-running studies into the adoption of innovative digital technology in incumbent organizations. After some six years of research, Swedish scholars Fredrik Svahn and Rikard Lindgren of the University of Gothenburg and Lars Mathiassen of Georgia State University published their findings in a paper entitled '*Embracing Digital Innovation in Incumbent Firms: How Volvo*

Cars Managed Competing Concerns' (Svahn, 2017). The study goes into detail about how Volvo Cars' managers balanced their options between running the 'old' business while introducing the 'new' business of in-car connectivity.

Since around 2010, digital technology has become a major competitive influence in the automotive market. Electronics have become as important as performance and comfort. And digital technology not only enhances users' experience; it also enables new revenue streams. To keep up the pace with development in electronics and digital technology, Volvo needed to rethink its traditional product development cycles. Volvo executives realized that this would not be easy to implement and would require fundamental changes in knowledge exchange, capabilities, processes and routines and the company's mindset and culture. And yet, at the same time they wanted to be careful not to do away with effective product development practices in non-digital functions that had been very successful to date.

Svahn's study centered around four competing concerns between the existing business and the digital business.

- Existing vs. new capabilities
- Product vs. process innovation
- Internal vs. external cooperation
- Control vs. flexible governance

Existing vs. requisite capabilities

In innovative environments, organizations develop new capabilities for product development and design, both technical capabilities, such as 3D printing or software development, and organizational capabilities, such as rapid prototyping and Lean Startup development. Such new capabilities may not align with or even contradict existing practices in product development. The new capabilities create tensions between employees that embrace change and those who want to (or feel required to) stick to old habits and rituals. Managing these tensions is pivotal in allowing effective responses to digital opportunities.

Product vs. process innovation

Digital technology shifts focus in innovation away from static incremental product improvement to creating digital platforms that can be continuously adapted and altered in real-time. Developing digital products and services inherently creates a requirement for continuous, short-cycled (agile) management processes. Such processes conflict with existing longer cycled processes, leaving challenges such as conflicting time horizons and resource distribution between process development and product development.

Internal vs. external cooperation

Digital technologies quickly broaden the scope of development to external partnerships and networks. While developing the internal skills required for digital transformation, organizations must also engage in external relationships and resources. When placing too much focus internally, managers might overlook important opportunities outside of the organization. However, when focusing too much on establishing partner networks they risk destabilizing internal work arrangements.

Control vs. flexible governance

As I will show in the next chapter, management must allow seemingly undirected creativity and research in search of digital opportunity, at the expense of existing systems of control and risk management. However, management is also responsible for the healthy operation and profitability of the incumbent firm. Accordingly, management must find a balance between control and flexibility to explore digital opportunities.

Volvo Cars' management achieved balance in these concerns through 'learning by doing,' or as the authors describe it "through an emergent tuning process of accommodation and resistance." Innovation at Volvo Cars had always been anchored in coordinated initiatives to improve car sales. Now, new digital technology led to the exploration of aftermarket opportunities for services. This caused both excitement and enthusiasm as well as frustration and friction. Management learned to sometimes stand fast and sometimes give way. To sometimes support the old and sometimes drive home the new. Even without making a choice for one or the other, the process led to an irreversible shift in both identity and organizational culture.

The study of Volvo Cars is interesting because it offers a unique insight into the growth path of a renowned industrial powerhouse moving from Plateau 1 to early Plateau 2. The balancing concerns of management also show that the wheels they have set in motion will lead to a further organizational change. Volvo's researchers conclude their finding with the suggestion that "a sustainable design vision [should be] at the heart of managerial intervention, whereas prior research depicts digital innovation as an emergent process wherein deliberate managerial intervention cannot help avoid unpredictable outcomes." This fully supports the notion in this book that, in order to move from Plateau 1 to Plateau 3, a vision on technology and market development is what turns unpredictable experimentation into a manageable process.

But vision alone will not get you there. Managing competing concerns requires practical and organizational skills in making choices, communicating them within the organization, and facilitating their requirements. During the research period, Volvo Cars has adopted characteristics of what is called 'organizational ambidexterity.' This refers to an organization's ability to simultaneously pursue both incremental improvement and innovation through formal, sometimes contradictory organizational structures and processes (and even cultures) within the same firm.

Think of the internal innovation lab or corporate startup, which usually hosts an entirely different way of working and corporate culture than the regular operation. Such ambidexterity allows the company to both exploit the old and explore the new at the same time through organized structures and processes, even though these may work as each other's opposites in achieving corporate goals. Although this may sound paradoxical, empirical evidence shows that this ambidexterity, "under conditions of market and technological uncertainty, [..] typically has a positive effect on firm performance." (O'Reilly, 2013) As you may recall from the Innovation Strategy Matrix, market and technological uncertainty are exactly what changes when organizations move from plateau to plateau.

There is no such thing as a blueprint for organizational ambidexterity. Just as there are no strict guidelines to adhere to when balancing competing concerns in digital innovation. The following chapters will therefore not outline 'how to become an ambidextrous organization in four easy steps.' They do, however, describe the practical implications of moving from Plateau 1 to Plateau 2 to Plateau 3.

CHAPTER 13
The Ambidextrous Organization

Innovation is as much about organizational
change as it is about technology

W hen Joseph Schumpeter died in 1950, the
world was only just beginning to recover
from World War II. Schumpeter did not live
to see how the same industrial power that
had powered the war effort on both sides was
now fueling a new gale of creative

destruction, just as he had described in his 1939 book. And how, just like he had predicted, the rise of mass production gave birth to the new world of consumerism.

In the 1950s, mass production of consumer goods created an immediate need for new types of organizations, focused on production optimization, economies of scale and, in order to control everything efficiently, standardization. With the increased capital locked in production capacity, this capacity became an increase in financial risk and with that came risk-mitigating measures. To ensure the quickest return on invested capital, more and more focus was placed on costs-management. Due to this, the late 1950s and early 1960's witnessed the birth of a new business expertise emerged in 'corporate strategy' and with it the first serious attention to structured cost accounting and production optimization. Fueled by consumerism and economic boom times in the '50s and '60s, corporations became bigger, more standardized and more averse to risk.

It worked exactly as Schumpeter had predicted: eventually, the organizational development from the craft shop into mass-producing concerns built-up pressure in the market, ready to be released by the next wave of creative destruction by entrepreneurs offering something new and improved and (most importantly) out of reach of risk-averse and sluggish incumbent producers. The cycle, although varying per industry, usually repeated anywhere between seven to eleven years.

When Harvard Business School professor Clayton Christensen published 'The Innovators Dilemma' in 1995, globalization and computerization had significantly reduced such cycle times. This was the era in which information technology experienced rapid growth, personal computers became useful and laptops became actually portable. It was the time in which the World Wide Web transformed the Internet from a place for nerds to a place for anyone. The web allowed for the unprecedented rapid sharing of ideas and knowledge.

As a result, everything seemed to go faster: innovation adoption curves, the pace at which a wide audience would start using new innovative products, started earlier and such technological innovation started disrupting incumbents so early on that it was almost impossible for them to defend. Incumbents, accustomed to strategies of 'operational excellence' and 'cost leadership,' could notice the establishment of new market entrants offering seemingly inferior products based on unproven technology.

Unwilling or unable to invest in the development of this (not so commercially interesting) technology, incumbents focused on their top clientele and maintaining a strategy of operational excellence, dictated by generating ROI on investments in assets. The disruptors, when growing their business in unprofitable segments, became able to improve their quality and service levels to the point where they could compete with the incumbents' offerings. The rise of the Internet worked very much in favor of the creative destructors, and it reduced the cycles of creative destruction to ranges of 5 years or less. Technological innovation was beginning to leave little room for generating an ROI on capital intensive assets in any reasonable timeframe.

Today, Schumpeter's business cycles have all but shrunk to zero. They have turned into a constant motion of change, fueled by on-demand availability of digital technologies, ubiquitous global communication, a highly skilled and globally available entrepreneurial talent pool, and immediate accessibility of venture capital.

In value chains, added value (or margin) is no longer proportional to the investments made in capital intensive assets, such as hardware and infrastructure. Margin value is more and more directly related to the investments in 'consumer experience;' services allowing for the interaction between a product and the consumer. Apps, chatbots, home-automation, in-car entertainment and Augmented Reality-applications are but a few generic examples. This 'right side of the value chain' is especially subject to digital technology innovation and therefore to change. This means that risk-averse behavior in relation to asset management (on the left side of the value chain) becomes especially harmful to incumbent strategies when it hampers competitive action on the right side of the value chain.

Different speeds for different processes

Digitization leads to a business environment in which change is near-constant. Increasingly, value is derived from the rapid adaptation to change, rather than from the optimization of asset management. Speed, rather than efficiency, is becoming the critical success factor in competition. But the organizational structures of most corporations today are still dictated by the risk aversion and optimization strategies that are directly related to asset investments. No matter how many digital products and services are developed and marketed, the asset investments are still best protected through high utilization rates (efficiency in operation) and a good degree of risk aversion. But this organizational design brings the pace of the organization down to the speed of the slowest denomination: the asset management business. The increasingly digitized service-part of the organization requires much greater flexibility and adaptiveness. In order to satisfy both concerns the corporation requires a bi-modal organization that can run at different speeds and that masters the skills and processes to balance them carefully.

Different mindsets and cultures

Obviously, bi-modal organizations are not born overnight. In most organizations, data-driven products and services usually spawn as innovative ideas and experiments. But as the Volvo Cars case showed, as soon as these ideas and experiments evolve into more structural products and services, their impact on the running business becomes bigger and causes strain. They push the organization towards the upper-right edge of Plateau 1.

However, the organizational mindset will not immediately consider reorganizing of splitting the fast-paced services business from the slower asset business. Instead, the natural response is to 'force the new into the existing mold.' Corporate culture tends to regard the status quo as the norm and will, for reasons of risk aversion and reluctance to change, try to adapt the innovation into existing processes and structures.

When this is not feasible or desirable, the new products and services are separated from the core, often in a 'corporate startup' or 'incubator,' where they can grow freely without obstructing the existing business. Without splitting the existing business into a bi-modal organization, the fast-moving digital services are separated in a split between the 'existing business' and 'future business.' In effect this is the first operationalization of the ambidextrous organization; an 'organization that has the ability to simultaneously pursue incremental improvement and innovation through formal, sometimes contradictory organizational structures and processes (and even cultures) within the same firm.'

However, while allowing more freedom to the innovative ideas, in reality, the separation also tends to increase the gap between the 'old' and the 'new.' In the long run, this leads to the core becoming less innovative, rather than more. Especially when the 'future business' gains traction at the expense of the 'existing business,' shareholders are likely to regard the innovation as an indirect destruction of capital; they will raise a debate based on short-term financial security, attempting to protect the much larger investments in the old business rather than favor the new.

To counter the physical separation of 'corporate startups,' ambidexterity in organizations can be improved through 'innovation labs,' where innovation is organized as a specific discipline and placed in a separate 'department.' Although the name 'lab' may suggest otherwise, in ambidextrous organizations these labs not only work to 'invent' new products and services, they are also responsible for working with the existing organization and external partners to either embed the new services into the existing portfolio or change the existing organization and/or partnership network to grow the innovation into a formal business.

When taking this one step further, we can pursue innovative ideas through specific innovation-oriented workflows, such as the concept of the 'Google Friday,' in which employees are allowed to spend a designated portion of their time on innovative ideas and improvements. The concept was popularized by Google, which, according to its 2004 IPO letter, allowed its employees to spend 20% of their time on what they think will most benefit Google. In reality, less than 10% of Google employees actually use this time, nevertheless the concept spawned very successful ideas such as Gmail and Google News. Since the concept became well-known, many companies have adopted the model of 'innovation-time' and even Lean and Agile workflow methods such as the Scaled Agile Framework incorporate 'free innovation time.'

The concept of innovation-oriented workflows does, however, require that the organizational structure and processes allow for (or even stimulate) a high degree of self-organization and agility. In many cases, the existing organization offers little room to maneuver for innovations and their supporting teams. Often the cadence of the regular workflow is too rigid, or the workload is too high to allow for the 'distractions' of a Google Friday or working with an innovation lab.

In other cases, the existing business regulations simply do not allow for 'deviation from the standard,' such as in oil & gas, where strict safety measures dictate processes, or in banking and insurance where legislation does not allow for experimental insurance offerings or credit ratings. In such situations, many companies choose to launch a 'corporate startup,' to create the required physical separation. It is important to keep in mind though, that this choice is a deliberate choice to accept the downsides of the separation as a cost to achieve the upsides of innovation. The organizational structure should by no means become the 'default landing zone' for all innovative ideas.

Each level of ambidexterity should find its own balance between resource allocation, the exchange of knowledge, speed of development, mindset, and culture. The key is to find just the right balance so that both the existing organization and the innovative organization operate as effectively as possible while keeping the ability to integrate back together when it is most beneficial. Not only is this a difficult exercise, it is an unending one. It requires a permanently fluid state of priority and preference between the different parts. Such a state requires permanent attention and does not allow easily for hierarchical solutions or rigid definitions of right and wrong. It is not surprising then that achieving ambidexterity is more difficult in traditional hierarchical organizations and is more easily achieved in Agile working environments.

Scaling up is hard to do

In my consulting practice, I have found that many large organizations have been relatively quick to pick up on the concept of innovation. Most have started their own concepts of free innovation time and innovation boosters, innovation labs and corporate startups. Although for many this has led to a steady flow of innovative ideas being developed to Minimum Viable Products, scaling up these concepts into a viable business and integrating them into the parent organization proves to be extremely difficult.

In many cases, promising ideas failed to mature because the parent organization had no good way of dealing with small, non-standard products and services. As a result, the ideas were forcefully absorbed into the parent framework in such a way that the innovation lost most of its innovative power, were neglected or, in the worst cases, were deliberately set up to fail. Apart from this being a waste of resources and energy, the loss of innovative power also means lost opportunities for future benefits and growth.

The entire concept of innovation is to introduce something new and then to adapt the enterprise to the new developments and allow to meet, or even lead, changing markets. Instead of operational efficiency and resilience to change, the organizations should embrace change and adapt to new ways of working based on the experiences of the development of the MVP. Don't get me wrong, I'm not proposing that organizations blindly adapt their structure and processes to small scale promises of future growth. But they should accommodate the growth of such promises and take tangible action to facilitate the integration of innovations into the parent structure. As we will discover in the following paragraphs, four areas, in particular, are key to the successful integration of innovations into the parent organization.

Merging the two flows

In May 2013, Charles O'Reilly III from Stanford University and Michael Tushman from Harvard Business School reviewed the then current state of research into 'organizational ambidexterity', covering 15 years of research on the topic (O'Reilly, 2013). They refer to organizational ambidexterity as 'the ability of an organization to both explore and exploit—to compete in mature technologies and markets where efficiency, control, and incremental improvement are prized and to also compete in new technologies and markets where flexibility, autonomy, and experimentation are needed.'

In their research, O'Reilly and Tushman point to what they call 'structural ambidexterity,' which *'entails not only separate structural units for exploration and exploitation but also different competencies, systems, incentives, processes, and cultures—each internally aligned.'* They conclude that although the most successful innovative organizations have separate activities for ideation and experimentation, they also focus on maintaining a *'common strategic intent, an overarching set of values, and targeted linking mechanisms to leverage shared assets.'*

In their view, the key to ambidexterity is *'the ability of an organization to sense and seize new opportunities through simultaneous exploration and exploitation. This is, at heart, a leadership issue more than a structural one.'* In my opinion, it is a bit too easy to dub ambidexterity a 'leadership issue', as this conclusion provides no hint to what or how leadership should decide in embedding innovations in the organization. In the same light, O'Reilly and Tushman continue to conclude that merging the two flows in ambidextrous organizations entails competencies, systems, incentives, processes, and cultures.

In today's business practice, this translates into the ability to continuously embed innovations into an organization's competencies, technology architecture, and processes. In addition to the research of O'Reilly, an increasingly important aspect of integrating innovations is the management of partnerships. As innovation is increasingly conducted in partnerships with suppliers and/or clients, managing the continuous integration of such partnerships in the organization becomes a core competence. Ambidexterity is a leadership issue in the sense that each of these areas' leadership must continuously manage the integration of innovations into the existing structure. They can do this by providing the mandate, bandwidth, and support for change of the existing organizational structure.

Technology architecture

Virtually all corporations develop and run their technology infrastructure based on what is called an 'Enterprise Architecture.' This architecture, in practice, translates to a set of principles and guidelines for the configuration of (new) technology. Enterprise Architecture safeguards the smooth (and cost-effective) integration and operation of the broad range of technologies that are in use in the enterprise.

Although a necessity for efficient operations, Enterprise Architecture is usually not designed to accommodate innovative technologies. Instead, it enforces a standard way of using proven technology. Implementing innovations, then, usually requires that the innovations are adapted to fit the existing architectural requirements. In most cases, this means that some or much of the powerful innovative capability of the innovation may be lost to standardization to an 'old' guideline. That may sound foolish and short-sighted, but this 'old' guideline serves an important purpose: it enables the standardization of technology with the aim to increase speed and efficiency in the IT landscape.

When the implementation of an innovation requires a change to the technology architecture, it directly threatens these goals of corporate agility and efficiency. It is therefore imperative that senior management and Enterprise Architects recognize the benefits of the individual innovation and allow for the adjustments of existing standards and requirements to accommodate the scale-up and embedding of it in the organization. Fortunately, recent developments in the field of Enterprise Architecture provide guidelines for this purpose, such as the principle of Agile Architecture, which balances the need for intentional architecture and emergent design. (Scaled Agile Inc., 2019)

Competencies

Innovations are as impactful as the people who work with them. Without competencies, the right skills and experience of people, innovations are mere technology or processes. Only with the right skills and experience can innovations enable competitive advantage. The buildup of competencies is pivotal to the successful embedding of an innovation. In fact, most people will only regard an innovation as 'embedded' when the competencies have become 'business-as-usual.' In this case, 'usual' implies experience and skill.

Successfully merging the two flows of the ambidextrous organization requires merging skills and experience of the 'old' way of working with the 'new' way of working, even when in some cases the innovation will replace the old way of working. Embedding innovations requires careful attention to developing new skills, recording and exchanging (new) experiences and lessons learned. It requires the careful build-up of a 'new usual' and assistance in the transfer of old to the new. It encompasses training of staff as well as supporting the decommissioning of old skills.

In terms of leadership in innovation, this means that senior management, rather than focus on achieving maximum efficiency, should focus on managing the most efficient transfer of skillsets and the creation of relevant and exploitable experience.

Many innovations fail not because they are bad or poorly executed ideas, but because they have not been properly embedded in the organization: the people who need to use the innovation have not been taught the required new skills, have not been 'untrained' old habits and/or have not been allowed enough time to build up experience and best practices.

Processes

After an innovation has outgrown the stage of experimentation, it needs to prove its value at scale. Although most attention in innovation literature goes out to early-stage experimentation and 'Lean Startup'-thinking, it is the scale-up phase in which the most pressing problems arise when sustaining the growth of innovations. It is during this stage that the innovation will come into conflict with business as usual.

During this scale-up phase, the innovation will prove its value through growth and impact. Subsequently, it will become clear that the innovation demands changes in existing processes and habits. It may even call for the replacement of existing products or services, potentially threatening successful ones. It is important to understand that the innovation should not be automatically adapted to the existing processes, but that the existing processes may need to be adapted to fit the requirements of the innovation to ensure sustainable impact. Since processes are the most tangible structure of an organization, senior management needs to actively mandate and guide such change of the existing organization, as it favors long term perspective over short term results.

Partnerships

Where startups have the relative luxury of focus on a single product with dedicated expertise, incumbents need to address multiple products, services, and markets at once. Although very powerful at mass production and managing complex go-to-market strategies, incumbents are not likely to be competitive at every aspect of innovation such as ideation and experimentation. In the same way, it is not likely that they can attract uniquely skilled staff in the same way that startups can. The only way for incumbents to remain competitive in an innovative landscape is to build bridges between breakthrough ideas, new technologies, and the corporation's power to mass-produce and go to market. Incumbents need to master the art of partnering, especially with organizations that are very different in size and skillsets.

Most incumbents already leverage partnerships with organizations of similar size and interests, such as suppliers, manufacturers, and (international) sales channels. Each of these partnerships serves as an almost direct extension of the incumbent. But partnerships in innovation are often very different: they focus on exchanging access to ideas and skills that are not readily available with the power and sales force of the incumbent. Managing such partnerships involves a systematic approach to assess how the partnership influences and drives value for both parties.

Reinventing KPIs

As I indicated in Chapter 8.1, , moving from Plateau 1 to Plateau 2 and beyond creates organizational strain. Data-driven products and services do not fit easily in existing performance indicators and do not easily match, or sometimes even outright contradict, existing targets. Consider the following example, which is based on a real-life case.

An Asian manufacturer of heavy equipment for mining and construction started equipping its trucks and machines with a broad variety of sensors. The sensors measure payloads in trucks and excavators, vehicle angles during loading and transport, engine performance, acceleration, and location.

The company developed multiple Plateau 1 services based on the sensor data. These services saved operating costs and reduced downtime through predictive maintenance, and increased safety through early tipping-over warnings and protection against overloading. The data-driven services were sold as add-on features to the trucks and, although successful, were not considered big money makers. In fact, the additional turnover generated was so low that management felt somewhat disappointed by the 'Internet-of-Things' opportunities that had carried such a big promise in the market.

In response to this disappointment, the product development team working on the sensor products wanted to rebuild the data management platform for the sensor data to be able to group data from multiple trucks into a 'customer fleet profile.' Such a profile would enable the company to advise customers on the optimization of the performance of their entire fleet rather than provide insights into the performance of individual trucks. Market research at multiple clients had indicated that such a fleet management service would be greatly appreciated.

The new service required additional investments in the data platform, in redesign of some sensors and in the refitting of sensors in some existing trucks. Senior management was reluctant to make this investment for a number of reasons. First and foremost, the margin on sensor products was reasonable, but servicing the sensors proved expensive and dependent on the cooperation of customers. In some cases, broken sensors were not replaced by customers. This was interpreted by the marketing team as though the sensor products delivered little value for money and that their fragility as harmful to the corporate brand image of 'reliability.'

Secondly, the return on investment of the data management platform proved difficult. The data services were offered and administrated under the existing maintenance subscription of each vehicle. The team tried to estimate how many clients would opt-in for the fleet management service and how many trucks per client would then be managed under that service. These assumptions were critical to being able to estimate the pricing for the fleet management service.

Historically, when new product features were developed in the company, the development costs of the feature were depreciated over a fixed time across all manufactured machines and as a consequence was calculated in the purchase price of the machine. The serviceable costs were then added to the maintenance subscription for each machine fitted with the feature.

The same strategy had been applied to the sensor products. The development costs of the data platform depreciated over a fixed time across all machines in the field and the operating costs of the sensor services were added to the maintenance subscription of each machine with the add-on sensor product.

For the fleet management platform, however, the depreciation costs were expected to place a disproportionate cost on the manufacturing price of new machines. Running costs of the service were difficult to administrate under the existing maintenance subscription and building a specific administrative module for the fleet management service would add even further to the depreciation costs.

During a heated debate about the matter in the management team meeting, the VP of marketing suggested to halt further development of the fleet management service until the sensor product had become more reliable. After all, he reasoned, there was no use in risking the brand name for products that were not adding to the bottom line.

The head of operations defended the digital offering by explaining that he was actively engaged with the IT department to hire and train new staff on setting up a digital service helpdesk to assist maintenance crews, fleet managers and drivers in using and improving the digital services.

The VP of sales, a respected veteran in the business, acted surprised when she heard about these unknown additional costs and suggested to increase the pricing of the sensor service subscription to maintain margin on the core offering, heavy equipment. She reasoned that the company had always managed to sell add-ons at a premium price compared to the base machine and wondered why digital products would need an exception to that rule.

The product development manager responsible for the digital services felt as if all eyes were on him to present an elegant solution to the problem. The CEO did not appear willing to allow him to make more promises for improvement in the future.

The product development manager decided to share part of a discussion he had had with his own team just days before. "It's ridiculous that they want to spread the development costs of the platform over newly sold machines in two years," one developer had said. "We are not building a machine add-on; we are building the foundation of an entirely new business."

A graduate student working on the project then asked an interesting question: "I don't see how this service is related to individual machines. Why do we try to administrate a fleet management service in the same system that is used for selling individual machines? Can we not just sell a subscription, administer it in Excel and then add data from trucks in our platform?" The product developer explained the vision from the sales department to his team. "To get data, the trucks need to have sensors and the customer needs to pay for those. And they need to pay a lot in order to keep the margin for the truck sales on par."

In an act of bravado, the student replied, "Then why don't *we* pay for the sensors on each truck and not sell them to the client. We can sell the service directly to the clients and not bore him or the sales team with this sensor-stuff at all. We don't want to make margin on sensors anyway. We want to make money on the analysis. We want to run our own platform business!"

"So," the development manager concluded his story to the management team, "perhaps we have been looking at this from the wrong angle. I suggest we try to see if we can set up the fleet management service as a new line of business and see if we can work around our own limitations in pricing and operations. I believe that, if we do not charge our clients for sensors, but for the fleet management service, within six months we can convert 60% of our clients from a free trial subscription to paying subscribers and run a profitable business within 24 months." He had formulated his own version of 'old processes x new technology = expensive operations' and concluded that new technology required its own efficient (i.e., ambidextrous) process *and* measures for success.

In the transition between Plateau 1 and Plateau 2, data-driven products and services come to require new performance indicators that transcend traditional success criteria. The primary reason is that data-driven services tend to overarch the implementation or usage of a single instance of a product. The strengths of such services lie exactly in the fact that data is not bound to a specific usage scenario, but can be analyzed across multiple product implementations, business lines, clients, periods of time, and can even be combined with third party data. Hence, determinants for costs, revenues, and profits and even for growth require the same overarching principles. Restraining the evaluation of the success of data-driven services to existing organizational habits and reporting structures will severely hamper their success.

Many managers will construe the need for separate KPIs as a structural weakness and incapability of the new technology to deliver value. After all, they argue, if we can't make decent money off it, why bother?

Recall Chapter 9's anecdote about the electricity provider VP who was worried that at the current linear rate of growth, his data business might require 11 years to match the turnover of the smallest business unit in the company? He had a realistic worry, even when not considering the unilateral standards for growth of corporate management. His solution to the problem, however, was not to decide on the matter based on his current perception of the market but based on his inability to predict future developments.

Just as afraid as he may have been about his team growing too slowly, he was afraid that the market for data services might grow exponentially, after which he would have been stuck with "300 employees in various departments who have the wrong education and skills." His definition of success was not to be found in turnover compared to other departments in the organization, but in growth compared to market development. Although the right approach, finding that metric turned out to be almost as hard as convincing senior management to adopt such a metric in the first place.

The importance of non-financial metrics

Financial data often proves to be insignificant when establishing the success ratio in immature or innovative markets. That is exactly why many startups and scale-ups adopt very different metrics: adoption rates of the service, conversion ratios from trial to paid subscription, and usage intensity in the field. Authors Benjamin Yoskovitz and Alistair Croll of "Lean Analytics: Use Data to Build a Better Startup Faster" (Yoskovitz, 2013) even go so far as to advise the use of something they call "the one metric that matters", which is a single, non-financial metric that best measures the momentum of the business you are in, the growth stage that your business is in and the audience you are targeting. According to Yoskovitz and Croll, the metric is:

1. A rate or a ratio. Absolute or cumulative figures blur the view of growth.

2. A comparison to a benchmark, such as a time period, a different group of users, and other countries.
3. "No more complicated than a golf handicap."

The purpose of the one metric that matters is for it to be discussed by people who can influence it. It is neither a measure of success nor a control mechanism. In innovative environments, metrics translate into action, not into bonus.

The authors make an interesting statement too about 'accounting metrics.' They should be "something which, when entered into your spreadsheet, makes your predictions more accurate." This last point is important because when moving from Plateau 1 to Plateau 2 you move more and more into uncharted territory: both your offering as the market in which you are offering it is new and unproven. The metrics used in data-driven service development should indicate your performance compared to benchmarks, such as the previous period, but also to establish your beliefs about the market potential.

Before accepting different metrics for a new line of data-driven business, senior management of the company will need to be convinced about the accuracy of market predictions, as it will need to be convinced about the service's business potential. However, business cases are usually built on assumptions derived from past experience.

In the example of the heavy equipment manufacturer, the case for data-driven business was built entirely on the business model for heavy equipment add-ons. Clearly, the new services did not measure up against that model. Yet the alternative, service-oriented business model was based entirely on assumptions and gut feelings. There simply was no experience or benchmark. Measuring turnover compared to existing business made no sense, as this was clearly a startup line of business. Measuring turnover growth was equally nugatory because of the short period and the limited number of active customers. Measuring profit... well.... next year....hopefully.

Evidently, the only measurement that could determine the success of the new line of business was the adoption rate of paying subscribers. That number could be used as a baseline to check the earlier assumptions on business growth. Influencing factors on the adoption rate, such as pricing, sales pitch, or service level, could be introduced to cross-check those growth assumptions and senior management could be informed about progress based on realistic predictions derived from practical experience.

The need for rapid iteration

If measurements are by default aimed at improving predictions, then they are equally by default aimed at indicating directions for next activities. After all, if the prediction turned out to be correct than we should continue on our way. However, if the predictions are incorrect, we need to adapt our expectations and change course.

In digital environments, data becomes available at a rapid pace and can be quickly analyzed and interpreted. And because the service is digital, changes can be implemented almost instantaneous. Prices of retail products can be adapted to customer's search behavior on the website. Logistics planning in warehouses can be adjusted based on actual sales figures from the organization at hourly intervals. Specifications for new products can be altered by analyzing real usage data from products in the field.   But we can only benefit from such opportunities if our organization is capable of changing directions equally fast. This is why successful digital businesses not only focus on their core development skills and data analytics but also on creating a highly adaptive and Agile organization that is ready to respond to whatever changes their data suggests.

CHAPTER 14
Agility Matters

The goal is to create an organization that can adapt to change without altering its structure

D
r Everett Rogers, author of the 1962 landmark study on innovation, *Diffusion of Innovations*, was born in 1931 on a farm in Iowa, United States. As a child, Rogers helped out on the farm and noticed how his father was keen on utilizing electrical and mechanical innovations in farming but proved very hesitant to use biological and chemical innovations. This reluctance somehow stuck in the young boy's head.

After obtaining his Ph.D. in rural sociology, Rogers tried to convince farmers to use a new strain of corn that promised much higher yields. He was met with the same reluctance he had witnessed in his father years earlier. It surprised him how most farmers would simply not accept his scientific word for it.

Over and over again farms rejected Rogers, until one day he met a young revolutionary who was willing to give it a try. The new strain proved highly successful, and Rogers was convinced that the other farmers would surely now believe him—but he was wrong. Although the crop results were convincing, the more traditional farmers were put off by Rogers' unorthodox business partner and snubbed him yet again.

The experience led Rogers to wonder why great ideas are not adopted, eventually leading him to publish his 1962 research, in which he categorized adoption of innovations by the market according to the speed at which groups start using the products. His categories were labeled 'innovators,' 'early adopters,' 'early majority,' 'late majority' and 'laggards.'

The theory of the diffusion of innovations is known to most business managers. On occasions, almost all of us consider ourselves to be 'innovators' or 'laggards'. What few realize is that the same principles apply 'inside' an organization trying to adopt new technology, a new way of working or a new business model.

Where incumbent organizations tend to become resistant to change for reasons of risk reduction and efficiency, a majority of people tend to be reluctant to change for any number of reasons, including fear of the unknown, a desire for (perceived) security through stability and perhaps even out of complacency. Entire libraries have been written about how to get people in organizations to change their behavior. Over the last four decades, change management has become an area of expertise in its own right, managing wave after wave of reorganizations, mergers, carve-outs, and other change initiators.

Most of such reorganizations focus on moving an organization from one fixed state into another, assuming that the to-be situation will fit the organizational purpose for the given next period. Yet with the increased speed of change over Schumpeter's *Gales of Creative Destruction* and Christensen's *Disruptive Innovations* it is unlikely that any new market status quo will remain for very long. The cost of reorganization must be paid—ideally, from the revenue boost that follows increased effectiveness and efficiency. So, with a declining time to earn back the investment, the business case for large scale organizational change is shrinking. At the same time the need to stay up to date with a modern organizational design is putting a bigger pressure on incumbents.

As a result, more and more companies are looking for an organizational form that will allow them to adapt to changing market circumstances without having to reorganize. Many find such a solution in what is called 'Agile' working. Over the last decade or two various 'new' forms of organizational and operational design have been experimented with and have proved successful in practice, such as Lean, Agile and the Scaled Agile Framework, Lean Startup, Holacracy, Semco Style and what has come to be known as the 'Spotify model.'

Although the focal points of each of these forms may differ, ranging from employee empowerment to responsiveness to change, most build on the same principles of organizing work around people rather than people around work. In most models, this leads to a dramatic reduction of hierarchy in favor of self-organizing teams and short, iterative production cycles. The 'new trick' involved in each of the models is about how prioritization of small batches of 'work to be done' is organized and coordinated amongst teams.

Some people may regard the above nothing short of business blasphemy, rolling up significantly different methods, models, and movements into the single term 'Agile.' But this book is neither about methodology nor about implementing organizational agility. More important than each method's advantages and disadvantages compared to one another is the overall idea of creating an organizational structure that focusses on continuous flow of work and adaptability to change. So, whenever I refer to 'Agile' in this chapter, I refer to the generic principles behind this idea.

Agile organizations do away with the idea that the company's process is stable. They do not strive for efficiency by grouping people with similar expertise per process step, such as a purchasing or sales department. Instead, they strive for adaptiveness by grouping people with different skills into teams and then carefully prioritizing the work that is done by the team. Although the work performed per employee is likely less efficient than in functional organizations, Agile organizations can very quickly adapt to new requirements or changing market conditions and significantly increase the speed at which output is produced. In increasingly digitized environments, such adaptiveness and speed are required even to keep up with market developments, let alone lead them. As explored in Chapter 9.5, '*Speed Trumps Efficiency*', Agile working is the way to realize Plateaus 2 and 3.

Agility is not optional

In the Innovation Strategy Matrix, following the roadmap from your existing Plateau 1 business to the data-driven Plateau 3 business models is a journey into unknown territory. It is by default a journey of discovery, gaining experience, changing views, and rescheduling plans. It is a journey of small steps rather than big plans and the absence of a reliable business case rather than plannable return on investment.

Incumbent organizations have difficulty getting to grips with small-scale, unfamiliar, innovative digital initiatives. Adapting rapidly to new insights is simply not in their risk-averse nature. Yet more and more of their business structure will be subject to rapid, innovative change. Business agility therefor is not optional, it is a required core capability for continuous innovation.

Iteratively develop products and services

At one point in our professional lives, we have all had the experience where we found out that the design or plan that we made did not quite live up to our expectations. You have probably uttered the sentence "well, it looked good on paper..." a few times yourself. If so, then you have probably also experienced the disappointment of having to do all of the rework needed to adapt the original product to the improved version.

Agile working, by default, accepts that no plan will deliver a perfect solution and tries to minimize the work done before a design is tested in practice. Products are developed by building the smallest possible working version and then testing it out. After each experience, improvements are added, and the product is tested again.

This way of working seems inefficient. After all, such continuous testing is expensive, time-consuming and confronts clients with incomplete products. Designing and building the whole product at once is easily more economical. Most of these arguments are actually true. Agile working is usually not cheaper than the traditional 'waterfall' way of designing, building, testing, and delivering a product in one run.

By comparison, after having invested the same amount of time and energy, Agile developed products and services have delivered more real market experience, match customer needs more closely and are of a higher quality level. In addition, by their iterative design, they are usually better equipped to facilitate adaptations and future design changes. Products developed in an Agile way deliver more value to clients more quickly. In an environment of rapid technological change with data as an unlimited and endless stream of raw material, that is not a competitive advantage, it is a competitive necessity.

When developing data-driven products in Plateau 1, Agile working adds another important advantage. By releasing small parts of the product often, employees that are not directly involved in the development process still become acquainted with the new technology early and frequently. They see effort and tangible results and learn to understand the workings of the data-driven products and services gradually.

Even though the initially delivered functionality may be underwhelming rather than overwhelming, it allows people to get comfortable with the concepts, vision, and goals and to get a 'common feel' of the effect it may have on their work in the future. One of the key success factors of breaking through the glass ceiling between Plateau 1 and 2 is a common understanding of the importance of data-driven solutions and a culture that supports continuous innovation. Iterative development of innovative solutions facilitates this common understanding and culture and a readiness to support change.

Work in multidisciplinary teams

Especially in incumbent organizations, the functional organizational structure (that is, the separation of departments by function: sales, marketing, production, IT) has led to a subconscious understanding that digital technology *supports* the business function. Traditionally, when we refer to 'IT' we are describing the people that are responsible for maintaining office hardware and software, such as laptops, CRM systems, and management reporting. Over the last decade, however, digital technology has become deeply intertwined with the business. ERP systems determine the workflow of knowledge workers in finance and administration, logistics systems automatically reorder parts used in production, websites have become primary sales channels, intelligent marketing automation systems send personalized messages to potential clients through Facebook and other social media.

Digital technology no longer supports the business—it *is* the business. The segregation between business and its perceived suppliers, in combination with the iterative development methods from the previous paragraph, causes difficulties in functional organizations. Short-cycled digital development requires extensive communication between many functional groups in an organization. Traditional interdepartmental handovers of work increasingly cause errors and delays and, in its wake, often a blame game between technology providers and users.

As an illustration of this idea, consider a fashion retailer operating physical stores and multiple online channels. Management decides to start selling shoes alongside its existing apparel offering. The new category has an impact on all aspects of the organization, including branding, store presentation, online sales, customer service, logistics, and finance reporting. Traditionally, category managers would decide which shoes to sell and then work with marketing to decide on branding and communication. Marketers would then order the web team to develop the new categories and content for the website and third-party websites. Store operations would then be asked to prepare the in-store presentation and logistics and eventually, the IT team would make the required changes to the ERP-system and management reports. The decision to sell shoes has tremendously impacted the work of all involved; the coordination of all these activities can cause more than a few headaches.

As you can see, most of the meetings scheduled in this project are not about the model, branding or pricing of the shoes involved, but about the coordination of efforts by all involved. Because we consequently describe each function in the company as a separate entity with its own tasks and responsibilities, we easily forget that each entity is closely linked to the other through interdependencies and systems.

Sales data from physical stores and the online channels form the basis of replenishment and back-orders in logistics. The same data is analyzed to discover the commercial impact of various ways of presenting the shoes in stores. Website data is used to determine which shoes are most frequently sold with which clothes and this data needs to be sent to stores for physical display and promotions. Online customers may wish to pick-up their shoes in a particular store. If a store is out of stock, an order might be delivered through the online channel, with the turnover appointed to the physical store. What appeared to be independent departments in a single production chain, more resembles a network of tasks in a system of different interactions with clients.

Agile organizations have adapted to resemble this network rather than the production chain. They organize into multidisciplinary teams representing members of each department, focusing on specific categories such as women's apparel or kids. Doing so greatly reduces the communication effort between each function. Obviously, coordination still remains between teams, but there is one important difference: multidisciplinary teams are focused directly on serving customer needs.

Functional teams tend to focus on being extremely good at their own thing: marketing, logistics, or finance. Multidisciplinary teams, on the other hand, have an intrinsic motivation to focus on customers: they are responsible for serving a particular segment. Marketing, logistics, and finance are all necessary components to serve the customer, and the team effort allows no deviation from that goal. There is no group emphasis on tasks, only on results. For each team this means that it can make its own quick adaptations to a website, it can quickly decide on which shoes to hold in stock, on which advice to give to stores on presentation. As mentioned, this process has its own coordination needs, but Agile companies in practice show that the Agile function of coordination is different to that of functional organizations. In functional organizations, coordination is required to keep the process flowing, in Agile organizations coordination is aimed at ensuring quality and consistency across the board. Even when coordination is sub-optimal, the process runs without delay.

Replace plans with planning

In most organizations, strategy is defined as the translation of a vision into a mission and related actionable, time-bound goals. The smallest being the 'annual budget,' usually safeguarded by quarterly reports. Although the default modus operandi of most organizations all of us know all too well that delivering on these goals, regardless of periodical reporting, is anything but straightforward.

The Agile movement responds in particular to flaws due to two assumptions made in this way of working: the first is that changes in the environment of the organization are predictable within the timeframe of a year and the second is that actionable, time-bound goals can be linearly translated into activities and their typical budgets. In practice, functional organizations tend to adapt to change through annual cycles of projects that are characterized by a fixed time and budget and a predefined scope: "we will develop and market this product in 6 months at a budget of US$2.1 million".

To allow for any unpredictability, the project plan usually consists of a pessimistic, a neutral, and an optimistic scenario. Progress is monitored by reviewing the development of the scope against the predefined budget at the given time. Whenever unexpected deviations from the plan occur, flexibility is created by changing either the allocated time (late delivery), the planned budget, or (in more cases than you might expect) quality of the delivered result.

Only on rare occasions do organizations decide to change the scope of the intended delivery (i.e., "within the given time and budget and with a dedicated quality level, we will deliver less than originally intended.") The reason is simple: once a project has started, it is very difficult to change the scope. It would be very difficult to stop developing and start marketing a product that is only half-finished, or to develop it as intended but then not to market it because the project had run out of money. These choices make no sense.

Therefore, when it has become clear that a project will run out of time or budget, there is nothing left but a choice between two evils; Stopping means losing all invested time and money. Continuing means spending more time (resources) and money. From that point onwards, management attention will focus on minimizing damage rather than on creating value. After all, other projects are waiting to use the precious resources in people and money that are stuck in the failed project.

In innovation, the vast majority of projects have a high degree of uncertainty and unpredictability with regards to what the final product will be, let alone how quickly it can be built and at what cost. Especially in the transition between Plateau 1 and 2, many projects suffer from a lack of frame-of-reference and corporate inexperience. So, planning any innovative project, with all of its assumptions about feasibility and value, based on a fixed scope solution in a fixed time and budget is an obvious pitfall. What are the chances of such a project actually arriving at the intended deliverable on time and on a budget?!

As we have seen before, the solution to this problem lies in the Agile approach of iterative development: building in small steps.

Limit the scope of the project to the smallest possible deliverable, build it, measure its effect, learn, and then build the next iteration. Projects do not last months, but only a few weeks. Each iteration, valuable lessons are translated into options for the future and an adjusted vision of the end result.

Management must learn to play an active role in the assessment of results and experiences in iterations of development. Based on these experiences, management can realign the vision with the experience or adjust the course of development.

In practice, most managers will argue that this type of monitoring is far too time-consuming. One common response might be: "Checking on the status of projects every two weeks? Surely something must be wrong with project management!" Traditionally, senior managers only get involved when things run off the rails or when key decisions need to be made.

This classic response of risk mitigation is actually very counterproductive when it comes to digital innovation. Spending time early and often to learn valuable lessons from real market feedback is far more valuable than spending time later on ill-informed decision making or, even worse, damage repair.

Even short cycled feedback and review do not immediately solve the problem, however, that most functional organizations adhere to annual planning and budgeting cycles. How can managers iteratively plan and budget new developments when all budgets have been allocated on November 1st of the previous year? Transitioning from measuring progress of plans to continuous planning of development activities requires one specific management   conviction: continuous   innovation   requires forward-thinking.

Digital innovations do not require a plan, but they do require careful planning. They do not require a fixed budget, but they do require available funds when development proves successful and valuable. They do not require a deadline, but they do require somebody knowledgeable to state when enough value has been delivered and time has come to direct resources and budget to achieving another goal. They do not require a system that instills a false sense of security upfront, but a system of transparency, communication, and trust that groups of people (not individuals) will make sensible decisions.

CHAPTER 15
Continuous Innovation

Innovation is not about generating ideas, it is about creating sustainable value

E ureka! An older man raises his arms in the air in excitement. His grey hair is in disarray, but it is not quite clear if this is caused by lack of care or by the static electricity involved in his last experiment. The white lab coat he is wearing flaps about when he rushes into the hallway, looking for people, although nobody in particular. He is excited because he has made a significant discovery. By the time he has reached the hallway his hands reach for his pockets, he realizes he has left his glasses on his desk, turns around and walks back into his lab, distracted by his own thoughts. His name could be Tesla, Marconi, Einstein, or Curie (in which case the man would be a woman, of course). The scene is all too familiar and for many epitomizes the word 'innovation.'

Alternatively, the setting might depict a group of youngsters on sofas using MacBooks covered in colorful stickers from hackathons, SXSW, and bands most people have not heard of. On the living room table are empty cans of energy drinks. Nobody cheers "Eureka!" because the significant discovery is disclosed to the rest of the people in the room via GitHub, with group-wide acknowledgements being made via Telegram using a thumbs-up emoticon.

Innovation is quite often mistaken for invention. Although the two are closely related, they are definitely not the same. Invention is the discovery of a new phenomenon, concept, or product. People invented the aircraft, solar panels and the small silicon valve that keeps liquids inside of a top-down bottle (unless when it is squeezed).

Innovation is not synonymous with invention; it covers the introduction of inventions in the market. Innovation is about applying inventions to achieve a particular goal. Aircraft enabled innovation in both passenger travel and in warfare. Solar panels caused innovation in energy production *and* in the production of clean drinking water in third world countries by enabling battery- and maintenance-free water filtering systems. And the silicon valve in bottles not only innovated the way NASA astronauts drink in space, but it also created an entirely new category of ketchup packaging, putting Heinz firmly in the lead.

Why is the distinction between invention and innovation so important? Because the idea that innovation is about the conception of novelties focusses the innovation discussion in organizations in the wrong direction. Clients frequently ask me how they can generate more innovative ideas. The question is understandable but nonetheless takes the wrong approach. Most companies have no shortage of ideas; they have a shortage of executive power in bringing such ideas to market. In a world where technological inventions rise and fall faster than pop songs, the problem is not so much in creating the idea but in bringing the possibilities to the market fast enough. The core competence required is not to have more mad scientists to create "Eureka!" moments. The key is to have people waiting in the hallway expecting the scientist to come out of his lab, who can support him in testing it in the market as quickly as possible, and then embedding it in the organization to leverage its value.

Continuous innovation as a core competence

Developing the organizational capability for continuous innovation requires a fundamental shift in thinking about how the business is organized, about how decisions are made, about partnerships and joint ventures and about the role of the management of such partnerships.

Incumbent organizations, as we have seen in chapter 5.1 *The Paradox of Asset-centric Business Models*, are organized in such a way as to minimize change. After all, change is expensive and bears risk. Incumbents prefer to churn out as many standardized products as possible to maximize the efficiency in processes. Whenever new products are brought to market, extensive preparation ensures that the product will meet the needs of the clients, will fit the processes and targets of existing sales and distribution channels, and meets the requirements of partners and resellers.

After a new product is invented, typically extensive market research will be conducted to test consumer demand. Then, based on the outcomes of the research, a business plan is developed and discussed and finally approved by management. The budget is allocated to set up design, production, produce stock, and distribute the product across the network of resellers. A marketing campaign is developed, and online and print materials are developed and distributed. Finally, the product is launched, and sales will take off... Hopefully. Fingers crossed.

Throughout this entire timeline, the product is being developed based on assumptions with no real market feedback. Moreover, the teams working on the introduction of the new product (product management, sales, marketing, and logistics) do so from the structure, perception, and culture of the existing organization. They work from what they know and will try to make the new product fit the existing company mold. In corporate reality, if the mad scientist had a real "Eureka!" moment and invented a Plateau 2 or 3 application, the existing process of design, production and marketing is more than likely to deform the original innovation into something that will fit the existing Plateau 1 organization.

In effect, the energy and time sent by business teams to bring the innovative product to market will be wasted. Not only because the new product will likely fail to materialize, but also because these teams have not been working on selling the existing product line. Even if new products are developed only a few times per year, this method of new product development is anything but efficient. In today's market, where new opportunities arise around the clock, a new model for bringing inventions to market is required. A model in which ideas are validated in the market by real customers as quickly as possible, where development is iterative and short cycled and where scale-up of production and marketing only happens when more paying clients adopt the product.

In such an environment, the focal point of innovation is not the product, but the process of innovation itself. This process is called 'continuous innovation'. Rather than starting a new project per innovation, in continuous innovation ideas follow a predetermined process of validation, experimentation, adaptation, scaling and embedding in the organization. It doesn't matter what the invention is, the process offers the quickest way to success or the earliest moment of failure.

The concept of continuous innovation is not unique to this book. Many great books have been written about the ability to continuously develop innovative products and services. What is striking about these publications is that they almost all to some degree refer to a way of working which has become the *de facto* way in which startups work; small multidisciplinary teams making iterative development of products based on rapid experimentation and real market feedback.

Eric Ries was one of the first to describe this way of working in *The Lean Startup*. In doing so, he set the standard for continuous innovation as a process. The book's successor, *The Startup Way* (Ries, 2017), is aimed especially at adopting the process *and* an entrepreneurial mindset and culture in incumbent businesses. Such a mindset is pivotal in organizations that offer Plateau 2 and 3 services but, as with any cultural change, it does not come overnight and cannot be taught through training. That is why the adoption of continuous innovation as a formalized process through Plateau 1, 2 and 3 not only helps to develop successful innovative new products and services, it also helps to change the corporate culture into a more entrepreneurial and agile one. Remember, the Innovation Strategy Matrix's horizontal axis is about adapting to the uncertainty of the market and organization. You may not be able to influence your market to a large extent, but you are in full control of your own organizational structure and culture.

Too often, organizational management focusses on creating new digital services and bringing them to market. Whenever an idea is brought forward, a project team is formed, development starts and when the product is finished, marketing launches a campaign, the sales force is trained, and the product is formally handed over to 'the business.' The 'business' receiving and accepting responsibility over this new product will demand that it complies to their current way of working. This is where incumbents differ greatly from startups. Startups do not have an organizational structure that is aimed at achieving other goals than the ones achievable through the innovation at hand. In most startups, the company's very mission is to launch the one innovative product it is working on. For incumbents, an innovation is a distraction from its running business. This is where for most incumbents the 'startup way of innovating' fails.

In addition to adopting the "startup way" of innovating, incumbents need to adopt a new way of *embedding* such innovations into the organization. Ideas should be continually generated and validated, iteratively developing them into valuable solutions. Those solutions must then be embedded in an organization that is adaptable to change. Rather than creating innovative products for the existing organization to sell, continuous innovation seeks to adapt the organization to fully leverage the market potential of innovations.

The Continuous Innovation Framework

Continuous innovation ought to a stable process in any organization and since 2018 I have been an active participant in the development of a publicly available blueprint for how to set it up in every organization. It is called the Continuous Innovation Framework (COIN) and its contents are available online at http://www.continuousinnovation.net. The framework is a body of knowledge that consists of five distinct areas of attention that need to be addressed in every organization in order to adopt continuous innovation:

- Ideation and Ownership
- Validation
- Experimentation

- Scaling
- Embedding

In the online version of the framework, each icon can be clicked for further explanation about the process step.

Ideation and ownership

One of the most overlooked issues in innovation is the ownership that people take over their original idea. There is no such thing as an innovative idea without anyone willing to bet on its outcome, against all odds. Why so melodramatic, you may ask? After all, if an innovative idea is so good, why would it have to be a bet 'against all odds'?

All too often, great ideas are brought forward by employees and are then quickly absorbed into the organization through project portfolio boards and the sincere enthusiasm of professional project managers. The point is that these entities operate within existing organizational guidelines and boundaries. Before long, innovative ideas will have to conform to business cases, promising designated returns on investment and provide planned stage-gate deliverables. Innovations do not work that way.

They are great ideas for novel ways of solving problems and adding customer value. They tend not to comply to existing ways of working and it is highly unlikely that a reliable prediction can be made about the exact workings of the idea, let alone its business case or its return on investment. For an innovative idea to prosper, the organization requires belief in its potential, not proof. That is why ownership is not easily transferrable from the person having the idea (the 'Innovator') to a detached professional performing his job. Both the job and the mindset will get in the way of success. The solution is to acknowledge the psychological ownership of the idea and facilitate the innovator to test and validate the idea in the real world. And in the process, transfer his ownership and enthusiasm to a larger group that can help to experiment and grow the idea to its full potential.

Leveraging the ownership of the idea is important because it drives people to defend the idea while simultaneously motivating others to change.

I have found in my consulting practice many times that nobody can pitch the idea better than the people who have come up with the idea in the first place. Their pitches combine a thorough understanding of the value that their idea delivers and of its inner workings. And more importantly, they have the tenacity to keep explaining the idea and convincing their colleagues and partners about the importance of them adopting the idea and changing their habits. In doing so, they set in motion the changes in the organization and in the corporate mindset necessary to embed the innovation in the organization in later stages.

Validation

An idea, even an innovative one, is just that: a representation of what may become a product, service and/or business model, contained within someone's mind. Innovation is about bringing ideas to life and turning them into tangible products, used by real clients.

As stated at the beginning of this chapter, popular theory of innovation features the startup as the ultimate form of organization for transitioning ideas into money-making products and services. The Lean Startup method of working centers around iterative experimentation: having an idea, building a Minimum Viable Product, testing it in the marketplace as quickly as possible, and adapting the design based on real customer feedback. The first step of in this way of working is, however, a paper exercise: the validation of the idea.

When they are still unrealized ideas, innovations are often exciting promises of new possibilities or remarkable technology. In the inspired pitches of innovators, potential problems and pitfalls in the realization of these promises are easily (or willingly) overlooked, too easily dismissed, or unintentionally avoided so as not to kill the dream. Validation is about getting everyone's feet back on the ground. About discovering omissions and assumptions in the idea that help to complete the idea from an initially inspiring thought to a well thought over the concept for innovation. Validation does not lead to a business case. Validation is also not about thinking through all scenarios and options. On the contrary, validation has nothing to do with planning at all. Validation is about envisioning the idea as a value creator. The aim is to look at the idea from both the angle of business and of technology and to prove or disprove the most important hypotheses that should be tested by the organization in a practical experiment.

Validation is desk research. It should happen very quickly, in a few days perhaps, by the Innovator and key stakeholders. Key questions to be answered in the validation phase are "Is it reasonable to assume that the product will work from a technical perspective? If so, what are the biggest challenges we will face in getting it to work?" and "How will the product deliver value to customers and is it reasonable to assume that we can capitalize on that value?"

The validation phase is usually conducted by a group of people discussing two topics: the product and the business model. The product is discussed with the objective to get a good univocal description of what the product is, albeit in broad terms. What does the product do? How will it work? How will customers use it? What specific technologies are required? How are they applied in the design? In addition, the group discusses how the product creates value for the customers. How does the product help customers to fulfill their needs, how often will they use it? Why is the product better than alternative solutions? The overview is not too detailed and should get everybody to be able to explain the product to third parties in a similar way. Most importantly, the validation phase is aimed at determining that it is reasonable to assume that the product can be built and that it offers customers competitive value for money.

Most new product development initiatives in incumbent organizations stop here. It is easily, almost automatically assumed that once the new product has been developed it will become part of the regular product catalog of the company, with salesforce and marketing picking up the challenges where required. However, as we have seen in this book, many data-driven solutions do not simply adhere to business-as-usual processes.

Products and services from Plateaus 2 and 3 require different market approaches, different organizational capabilities, and different business models. This is why it is imperative to develop an understanding of the business model by which the new product will be marketed. The objective of the validation phase is not to prove that building the product is feasible and most certainly not to develop a business case. The objective is to create a common understanding of the workings of the product and the mechanism of the business model.

One of my clients describes the objective of the validation phase as 'to make a reasonably substantiated claim that the idea may add value to the company in at least one of its strategic objectives within five years.' The validation holds no claim to costs or return on investment. It simply ensures that everybody has the same thing in mind when the idea is discussed, that everyone in the company can have a reasonable idea about the value it will deliver and through which business model it will reap its benefits.

The tangible result of the validation phase is the definition of a first experiment to test the most important hypothesis derived from the validation. For the innovator, this result is the stage-gate to innovation budget. Every innovator who has been supported by a corporate 'innovation coach' in the validation phase automatically receives a budget of max. €25,000 (or approximately US$29,000) to complete the first experiment within 12 weeks.

Experimentation

A famous quote by Nobel laureate Ronald Coase reads "if you torture data long enough, it will confess [to anything]." In much the same way, over-validation and theoretical design and planning of innovative ideas and their business potential will eventually lead to fantastic prognoses for future revenue that are utterly unreliable. There is but one way to test an innovation and that is to put it in the market and measure results. I have explained before, it is imperative to start such tests as early as possible. Rather than build and test the completely finished product, it is far smarter, cheaper, and faster to start tests using a minimum viable product, collect feedback from real customers and build what people want, not what you think they want. It is sometimes prudent to run important experiments even before creating an MVP.

This is why the tangible result of the validation phase is the preparation from the experimentation phase. The validation phase identifies assumptions that people make when describing the workings of the product or its business model. These assumptions can be ranked by the impact that they have on the realization of the innovation. The assumption that has the biggest impact when proven wrong is called the biggest *fail factor*.

Typically, the first experiment to run with an innovation is an experiment that tests this assumption. When I worked with a large bank to develop highly targeted mortgage services, the idea came from market research that indicated that customers were often highly sensitive to peer behavior. The idea assumed that prospects would highly value knowing the behavior of the majority of their peers when selecting financial products and services.

The innovation was to offer clients personalized advice by showing them the mortgage type chosen by other people who had demonstrated similar lifestyles and spending patterns. The innovators had come to describe the product as 'the financial equivalent of Amazon book recommendations': "people who bought this book also bought..." During the validation phase, a number of assumptions were detected in the product definition and the business model. Although the complex 'recommender algorithm' was regarded as a major challenge to build, the biggest *fail factor* that was identified was the assumption that people would feel threatened in their privacy by the comparison of their financial data to others.

The first experiment performed by the innovation team was to create a mockup of the personalized mortgage advice using

PowerPoint. Then, two employees of the company went to the nearest shopping mall to demonstrate the mortgage advice site on an iPad to passers-by fitting the description of the target group. The results were quite unexpected. Although people were adamant that the system should protect their privacy, they would quite quickly assume that the bank would guarantee this. The unexpected thing was that most people stated they were interested not only in which choices their peers had made, but in the reasons behind those choses. When asked if they would provide their motivation for particular choices in exchange for being able to see that of peers, the majority of interviewees answered positively.

Without programming a single line of code, the initial experiment had proven two things: the biggest fail factor did not exist, and customers had pointed to the real value of the service even before it had been properly designed. It had also provided for the hypothesis to be tested in the next experiment: "We can create a simple user interface to capture and compare motivations for choices for specific mortgage services." Again, mockups were used, but this time proving the hypothesis turned out to be far from easy....

Running such experiments is a great way to iteratively develop a product or service based on real customer feedback. This is not only because they focus directly on customer feedback, but because they offer a very rewarding way of working. Experiments are short, mostly between four and six weeks. They are based on clear and easy to understand working methods, such as Value Proposition Design by Alexander Osterwalder (author the famous Business Model Canvas) or adapted versions of

Scrum, the development practice of Agile teams, usually mingled with principles from Eric Ries' *The Lean Startup*.

This makes innovation experiments transparent, fast-paced and almost impervious to politics and power play. Experiments are, therefore, exciting. This is why many startups have institutionalized experimentation into the default way of working. For them, experimentation is not a phase; continuous iteration and constant improvement are how the company develops products. This *modus operandi* is not only attractive, it actually works for most startups.

Surprisingly, the experimentation method also works for most non-digital products. Continuous experimentation has worked for developing cars, lighting systems, financial products, gas turbines, and heating systems. This method, though, is not a guarantee for success. For many incumbents, the concept of continued experimentation to develop new products leads to failure.

Contrary to technology startups, which usually achieve great momentum through experimentation, incumbents that experiment for too long tend to lose that momentum, even when the product gains traction in the market. It is as if the organization at some point simply loses interest and gives up, regardless of results. The product ownership is transferred to a specific department, the original development team is disbanded because of priorities elsewhere and before long sales plummet and the product is side-tracked.

There are two distinct reasons why incumbents are not very good at continued experimentation. First, the incumbent development team cannot maintain ownership of the product and grow with it. In startups, if the product becomes a success, the company grows with it. The people that created the product in the first place become responsible for managing the ecosystem surrounding the product.

Incumbents already have an ecosystem in place. An entire organization exists, with its own marketing and sales and logistics and other protocols, that is not geared towards growing a single product but towards managing a portfolio of products. In the transition of the product from the development team to the running operation, early experience and "market feel" get lost. The product often turns out to be insufficiently self-supporting to be maintained by a detached organization.

The second reason is that continued experimentation hampers scaling up. Experimentation placed emphasis on developing customer value, most often translated into features of the product. For startups, feature usage is often an indicator of success and growth. Even if the absolute number of users is low, the adoption rate of the product or new features is a leading indicator of achievement. For startups, company growth is linear to product adoption in the market. Experimentation to improve features works very well in that situation. In incumbents, size matters. For any product to be successful, a particular turnover volume or customer base is required quite early on in the innovation process. The organizational structures such as sales, marketing, and logistics require a minimum volume to become effective and economical.

If the company cannot scale the volume to this 'organizational minimum,' the innovation will be incompatible. Even when growth rates are impressive, if minimum volumes are not met, the innovation will be terminated. So early on in the innovation phase, attention is required to scaling up the initiative rather than to improve the product. In many incumbents, this is quite paradoxical, since scaling up sales & marketing activity for an 'unfinished' product is just not done. However, it is advisable to limit the number of experiments that may be performed to develop the core functionality of the innovation before scaling up the initiative. It is this inflection point that creates the difference between placing emphasis on the word 'innovation' or on the word 'continuous.'

Over the last few years, corporate innovation has drawn a lot of attention, with many corporations launching innovation labs, incubators, and corporate startups. Most of these initiatives have focused on 'innovation,' which in practice has translated to new product development. Although many successful products have been introduced to the market, remarkably few have significantly added to the bottom line of their incumbent parent.

If, on the other hand, the focus is placed on the word 'continuous,' the role of the experimentation phase changes dramatically. The purpose of this book is to explain how data and digital technology impact the existing ways of working in incumbent organizations. It is about creating a way to continuously be able to take an innovative idea or technological opportunity and develop it into a proposition that creates customer value.

Incumbents have a natural tendency to reject anything that does not match the current processes that are in place to achieve optimal efficiency. Starting a corporate lab or other forms of externalized innovation machine is the traditional response to resistance to change. The argument that a corporate startup 'outside of headquarters' will keep the innovation safe from the 'old-fashioned, hindering parent' also means that the exact opposite does not occur: the old-fashioned, hindering parent will not learn a thing from what is achieved by the startup.

In the long run, those lessons will prove to be far more valuable than the short-term products and services that the startup invents. Hence, the experimentation phase should not only be aimed at experimenting with the product, but also with the introduction of the product into the market by means of the incumbent organization. Striving for 'continuous innovation' means that the organization learns to handle a continuous stream of experimental products and services and finds a predictable and stable process to transform them into a scalable new product line.

In my consulting practice, I have found that a period of about 18 weeks is usually a maximum stretch for the experimentation phase. This period is derived from three experiments, each lasting 6 weeks in which the experiment is set up, performed, and evaluated. Since most companies do not have staff available full-time to work on innovations, project teams are formed to work on the experimentation phases part-time, usually for 1 or 2 days per week for some defined period of time. What I have found is that such teams mostly can last up to 18 weeks before being disbanded and reassigned to other priorities. The arguments to disband vary, but usually, include the fact that 'other projects are waiting for development capacity' or that 'we have reached the point where we need a solid business case and approval by the project management board before we can invest any further.'

Innovators will immediately frown upon such arguments and protest: "we will not develop a business case because it would be based on nothing but assumptions and writing such nonsense and trusting on it would pose a greater risk to losing money and time than experimental development. This is why we use a structured process of iterative experimentation to test these assumptions in the real market rather than spend time and energy on creating spreadsheets that will cost us as much time and money and cause a delay in the development process without proving anything." I couldn't agree more with this counter-argument. But there is one thing to be said for the request to prove a business case before allocating more budget and (usually more strenuous) resources. The experimentation phase is quite easily focused on developing product features and design. The aim is to build what customers want and use in practice. But most incumbent organizations are not gearing up towards adopting the best possible product, they need to prepare to roll the product out to the market and sell a lot of it. The natural focus of an incumbent organization is to leverage scale before anything else and scaling up can be a serious blocking issue to the iterative development cycle of innovative products.

Developing an organization capable of continuous innovation requires that management and innovators alike recognize that focus in the experimentation phase shifts from proving customer value to proving the ability to scale. It is pivotal for continued success that they understand that from this inflection point their core task is no longer to manage the product but to manage its introduction into the market using the existing organization's strengths. The competitive battle between startups and incumbents is not in their equal capability to invent products, it is to bring them to market and to own that market. In early-stage development, startups have the natural upper hand because of their relentless focus on one product and the ability to grow and model their entire organization around that product. Most incumbents try their utmost to mimic this behavior, cheered on by popular belief that 'the startup way' is the only right way. They ought not to forget that they, the incumbents, have the upper hand in the scaling up of the initiative and should recognize and institutionalize the earliest possible moment to leverage scale.

Scaling

So, when it comes to innovation, the competitive power of incumbents lies in scale. Incumbents may be beaten by startups in quickly developing disruptive concepts, they dominate when it comes to market ownership. As I have shown in chapter 0 '*Installed base trumps everything*', scale translates into marketing impact, sales power, distribution speed, retail power, and many more advantages. Scale brings spending power and reach.

On the other hand, scale also brings a disposition to *act* at scale. Large organizations cannot handle small initiatives at an efficient cost. Processes and systems are all geared towards volume and will not efficiently handle small batches. Imagine Nike having to sell no more than 1,000 pairs of shoes designed by famous basketball player Lebron James. Just think of the consequences of distributing these shoes to the more than 1,150 Nike operated stores in 45 countries.

Which stores will not get a pair? And how do we ship a single shoebox to each store at an affordable cost? The company might be able to pull this off as a large-scale publicity campaign, with a dedicated marketing department handling all the logistics. Generally speaking, though, selling so few products through its original sales and logistics channels would be a nightmare. Nike is about big retail, not about small batches, even when it comes to innovations in sports apparel. Whenever innovative products are launched in incumbent organizations, they are required to sell in significant numbers from the start, if only to demonstrate their future potential.

In his book '*Velocity*,' Nike VP of Digital Sports Stefan Olander recounts the company developing its Nike Plus digital platform, together with Steve Jobs at Apple. The first questions that the team seeks to answer are '1. Does it help athletes get better?' and '2. Does it have the potential to add a million new members?' Scale was right behind customer value (Ajaz, 2012).

This is why attention must be turned to scaling up market coverage as soon as experimentation demonstrates viability. Digital services, when scaled, develop different characteristics than their smaller origins. Functionally, they require different technical management such as larger server capacity, performance monitoring, and load balancing. Yet they also become subject to less obvious changes in the behavior of technology and clients. These changes follow some mathematical laws of physics that control growth in both the physical world, in political networks and corporate organisms. The how-and-why of these changes are quite eloquently explained by theoretical physicist Geoffrey West in his book '*Scale*' (West, 2017). West explains that economies of scale happen in every type of organism, biological or organizational. Much like in animals the body mass increases exponentially with size, in cities the number of gas stations per capita decreases when the city doubles in size and the crime rate per capita increases. (West, 2017).

In a very similar way, analyzing expanding datasets will lead to different algorithm behavior for different sizes of datasets. Adding more clients to the systems will lead to a greater variation of unexpected problems, questions and new value-creating opportunities. In itself, this is not revelatory. But put together a new type of product or service which has not yet been completely developed, introduced as a novelty into a market by a team that has virtually no experience with it, knowing that the product itself will start to change its behavior after introduction in the market, and that quickly sounds like a recipe for disaster.

Fortunately, scaling the innovation (with innovation meaning not just the new product, but the new product introduced in the market) adheres to the same principles of the Lean Startup cycle of Build, Measure and Learn. Except in this case, we can read 'build' either as 'adding new features' or as 'changing the delivery of those features.' And we do not complete the cycle with a small development team, but with an increasing spread of functions in the organization.

Effective scaling up of an innovation hinges in a fast and effective feedback loop. Where the experimentation phase feedback was quite direct from a small group of clients, during scale-up, feedback typically increases in quantity and decreases in quality. As such, great attention must be paid to the automatic garnering of real usage data, and the translation of this data into usable statistics and insights. In addition, the data should be analyzed to suggest improvements to KPIs much different from the ones used in experimentation: During experiments, the focus was on finding customer value delivered by the product. In the scale-up phase, KPIs should be aimed at measuring growth of adoption. Examples of such indicators include:

- The number of new users per week
- The retention ratio for new clients
- The conversion ratio from free to paid subscriptions
- The number of referrals by existing clients
- The growth of average time spent using the product

During this stage, it will become more apparent that different teams in the incumbent need to work together to achieve result. Marketing, operations, customer support are all confronted with the impact of the new service. In Chapters 7 and 8, I referred to a case of a publisher, where I worked to introduce personalized news services, with both editorial content and advertisements being based on the previous reading behavior of clients. The program was relatively easy to set up when defining the initial experiments.

The advertising sales department was represented by enthusiastic young commercialists who recognized the potential for selling premium advertising space. The editors representing the editorial staff regarded the experiments as just that: experiments and were open to ideas although somewhat skeptical about algorithms determining what readers would like. And the branding and subscription sales team were excited about the potential to continuously perform A/B tests to offer ever more tailored subscription plans.

Even within 6 weeks the results of advertising sales looked promising, average page view times increased and subscription conversion went up for the test groups. Senior management was impressed, but when the time came to scale up things became difficult. Scaling up required more coordination between teams, uncovered technical difficulties in connection operational systems and, as the technology went from a protected test-environment into the public operational environment, more attention to protect consumer privacy. It also turned out that on a larger scale, advertisers were not able to deliver the creative material for each target audience on time and that a new, personalized online subscription product might cannibalize existing print subscriptions.

What looked like a certain business case in experiments was not straightforward in practice. When management decided to solve these scaling problems by handing the execution of the program to 'the business,' each department took responsibility of its own expertise and a large part of the innovations were lost through neglect. Had the company spent more time on the scaling phase of the innovations, the embedding of the innovations in the organization would have been more successful.

The scaling phase is the first phase in which the organizational change caused by innovations becomes apparent. It is the phase where the glass ceiling is broken, and the innovation moves from Plateau 1 to Plateau 2. Organizational change does not necessarily mean that existing departments and structures need to be disbanded or restructured. It does mean that more people need to work across silos striving for performance targets that are not necessarily in line with departmental goals. This means that the scaling phase requires not only serious management attention, but active management push to turn experiments into viable business opportunities.

Embedding

It is easy to think that when an innovation starts to gain traction, all in the organization will flock to support this new and exciting success. Well, it doesn't – not by a long shot. As you probably have experienced yourself, many will actively resist the adoption of innovations, to some degree. The fact of the matter is that people, in general, are not very keen on change. Change brings uncertainty, puts us off balance, and forces us to rethink our relationships with others. By nature, these are threatening situations for people and for organizations alike.

Most large organizations are risk-averse by nature because they aim to achieve extreme efficiency in order to generate the highest possible margin. This strategy demands a steady operational course for a certain period of time in which the efficiency can have its effect. Such a stable period matches the theories of both Schumpeter's business cycles and Christensen's disruptive innovations, which predict a stable business environment for roughly 10 and 5 years, respectively.

These theories have become the norms, to the extent that the organizational blueprints of most incumbent's support stability rather than change. By design, incumbent organizations tend to resist innovation and this resistance is deeply engrained in our corporate culture. Changing this corporate culture to support continuous innovation is going to be anything but easy.

A popular maxim in business supports this notion by stating that 'culture eats strategy for breakfast.'[5] Even when an innovation picks up momentum, there is no reason to assume that the standing organization is likely to adopt it in its core operations and processes. Even when successful in the market innovations can still be denied by the organization if they do not support the existing culture and views. An active policy of embedding the innovation and the changes that it brings with it is required to secure its future.

The very reason why incumbents should pursue a strategy of phased introduction of innovations from Plateau 1 to Plateau 3 is that it creates a culture where continuous change is the norm rather than the disruptor of stability. Such a norm is often only perceived as such if it is reflected in targets and management reporting. From that perspective, innovation can be considered 'embedded' when the key indicators for the measurement of

---

[5] The quote is often misattributed to Peter Drucker, yet it is most likely a popular rephrasing of an old adage "culture beats strategy" from a 2000 publication by the Giga Information Group.

success for that innovation are supported upwards along the chain of command.

Around 2010, at Volvo Cars in Sweden, a team of innovators had been working frantically to support a management vision that digital technology could somehow 'give life' to a car beyond its production. The vision was that digital technology could enhance the end-user experience and open up new revenue streams by selling and adding new digital features to cars on the road, either through dealer service or through direct download via the Internet.

The innovators decided upon developing a generic software platform that could serve as a launching pad for functions that could be designed at a later time and perhaps even by different vendors. This posed a challenge for the innovators since up until that point functionalities in cars were designed up to four years ahead of production time. The idea of a single platform created considerable pushback from the organization.

What good was all this talking about a platform? Which specific functions would it bring and when would they become an integral part of new cars? Middle managers, especially, felt trapped between the innovative capabilities supporting management's long-term vision and the short-term commitments that the same management demanded from existing practices. In great part, the short-term commitment was driven by risk aversity. The company had traditionally relied on early selection of technologies and functions for its next generation of products but making decisions about features on a connected car platform four years in advance seemed naive.

In order to embed innovation in the organizational culture, Volvo needed to develop new capabilities for delayed decision-making. The innovation team first achieved this through extensive discussion and collaboration with engineers and product managers. These discussions led to a broader understanding of the potential of the new platform.

Secondly, Volvo management learnt to shift setting target away from the outcome of innovation projects, such as return on investment on a particular technology, to the outcome of the innovation process; how many projects have we started and completed, regardless of their success. Volvo continued to experiment and use the platform for existing functions on the one hand and to reinforce innovation in the other hand, with management actively demanding results in both fields and stimulating the discussions and information exchange.

Over time, the connected car platform developed to a broader range of applications—not just as a product platform, but also as a business model for multi-sided markets, servicing both drivers of cars and external parties offering services on the platform. One such service was the 'Roam Delivery Service,' through which drivers could share their digital key with couriers to allow them to deliver parcels directly into their parked car.

Volvo management successfully embedded innovations into the organization not by setting targets on individual implementations, but by embedding a culture of change and by balancing risk versus forward-thinking. From that culture, adopting innovative technology became the sensible thing to do for all teams, not just the innovation team. The role of the innovation team changed from a responsibility to create innovations to a responsibility to support the entire organization in the rapid and frictionless adoption of innovations in the core process.

If successful embedding of innovations is dependent on the creation of the right incentives and targets by management, line managers will immediately be impacted. They will find that, when pursuing such targets, their existing resources are often insufficient for the adoption of a novel technology or process. Change demands capacity to realign existing activities and balance the new and the old.

No matter how hard an organization plans the transition from the old to the new, there is no such thing as flawless change. So much so, in fact, that organizations that have become exceptional at continuous innovation, do away with the notion of planning change altogether. Instead, they plan efficient availability of change capacity at any time, at any point in the organization. This is easier said than done, however. How do you plan consistent availability of resources of you cannot determine the required expertise nor the time at which it is required?

If experimentation and scaling of innovations are about building a solution and running a relatively predictable number of development iterations, the embedding phase is far more about making adjustments in both the existing and the new processes. It is about troubleshooting and creating efficiency. It is about quickly resolving any friction that may delay the adoption of the innovation (and with it the realization of the intended benefits).

Strangely enough, up until this point most organizations expect and plan for almost instantaneous results from the innovation.

This is usually because one or more business case spreadsheets calculated benefits to be effective from the month the innovation was supposed to be 'live.' In reality, the innovations do not deliver all of their intended benefits from day one; embedding them requires additional time and effort, but from whom and when proves difficult to predict.

Time must be spent on resolving unpredictable friction, such as making changes to existing IT systems, integration of services with third parties, managing unexpected training needs, and additional communication efforts. The people asked to expend this time are usually not in the scope of management of the department that needs their service. This puts the effective embedding of the innovation in the hands of those who have only a partial interest in its success.

This is why the task of embedding innovations should be allocated to a multidisciplinary team of senior managers who can allocate ad-hoc capacity to adapt existing processes and address unexpected needs. Because of its multidisciplinary nature, the team can effectively and decisively allocate resources weighing the company interest against each departmental interest. At the same time, they can monitor progress of the embedding of the innovation and the development of its intended benefits.

In most organizations, such a team already functions as an 'innovation governance board' or 'steering committee.' By extending the responsibilities of this board to a timely removal of friction and effective embedding, its participants can and will take an active part in allocating resources to solve problems. This resource allocation means switching priorities from the regular project portfolio to the embedding of innovations, where the innovations require no additional business case or planning. This will delay the implementation of projects in the corporate portfolio, but by using Agile methods of value calculation, such as Cost of Delay and prioritization, such as Weighted Shortest Job First, the benefit of such a switch can be made transparent. And they usually turn out to suggest prioritizing embedding innovations over delaying a running project, since innovations at this stage represent a greater investment of time and money, which is closer to delivering value than the running project.

The definition of success is 'flow'

Recently I was discussing the topic of innovation with a senior executive at a large software company. The company, active in a niche market, holds well over 50% market share with three dominant competitors sharing the other half. When discussing the importance of innovation, he looked at me and said, "We are increasingly experiencing competition from companies outside our domain, such as big tech companies like Google and Facebook and small digital natives. They offer some really smart services and are eating away our margin without taking over the complexity. Don't get me wrong, we have great people on board. We are a very smart company indeed. We are successful and very profitable, but 30 years of continuous growth has not taught us to be fast. We have become fat and complacent. And now digital technology will make us play the game against an infinite number of competitors, including our own clients."

Apparently, even for software companies, digital disruption is a threat. To prove it, the executive had rebranded his department from 'R&D' to 'Digital,' a name that put a smile on my face. What else to call it?

Digital technology is extremely versatile, has a very low barrier to entry, and can be easily scaled to serve a large market. It makes it easy to turn a creative idea into a working solution and deliver it to a global audience. For incumbents, this means that they have many more ideas to try and less time to try them It just isn't good enough anymore to set up and launch a project organization to evaluate an innovative idea once it surfaces.

 In this day and age, organizations should generate a continuous influx of ideas and operate a reliable and available process to take the ideas, evaluate and adopt them. The aim of the process is not to assess and develop the particular value of a single idea in light of the existing organization, but to process all available ideas and select and develop the ones with short term and long-term strategic potential. This process is called 'continuous innovation'.

Continuous Innovation is a process competence rather than a technology competence. It is much more about creating flow than about creating the next big thing. As a result, the key metric for continuous innovation is not the number of ideas processed, but the number of ideas processed *per given period*. Some may argue that the primary measure for innovation success is the value delivered by the innovations, and they are quite right. But measuring the value contribution of a particular innovation is not only extremely difficult, it also takes time.

Ultimately, the product needs to be introduced into the market in significant numbers to generate usable statistics about its value contribution. Especially in the early stages of innovation, development of validation and experimentation the measurable value contribution of an innovation will low and future potential will be debatable. Putting in place elaborate steering mechanisms for measuring and assessing value delivery in those stages of the innovation process tends to slow down the process. Such mechanisms often try to overcome uncertainty by adding administrative layers of data collection and reporting that slow down the system and do not actually reduce risk.

Instead, it is better to focus on increasing the flow of ideas through the stages. A steady flow through the innovation funnel actually does increase value delivery in two ways: First, it keeps ideas as small as possible. Small products are easier to build, test, and bring to real users for feedback. This feedback is the only dependable indicator for value delivery and allows teams to build more valuable products and services. Second, flow decreases the time to market of ideas. This is important because this means that value will start to flow to the organization sooner and scale-up can take place earlier. In financial terms, this means that the return on investment will be faster and higher as the accumulated income grows.

Flow optimization requires active management of the innovation process. In the Continuous Innovation Framework, innovators may be the greatest supporters of their idea; this does not mean that they are automatically geared towards the fastest possible development of their idea into a Minimum Viable Product. On the contrary, many innovators tend to first develop their idea to perfection before releasing it to the market. Their drive to build more counters the need to release fast and often.

It is therefore imperative that an "outsider" to the team coaches the innovators to build and release in small iterations, safeguarding the rapid flow of ideas into experiments and embedding these in the organization. This support allows the innovators to keep focus on quality, while the coach steers to maintain pace. Successful organizations employ such 'innovation coaches' with the explicit goals to optimize flow through active coaching of innovators.

Slicing big innovations into smaller pieces is not the only way through which such coaches can optimize flow. Often a major constraint in the flow is formed by the availability of management to dedicate resources and funds to the many ideas in the funnel. As I showed in the previous section, a multidisciplinary team of senior managers (the 'Continuous Innovation Board') should facilitate the cross-domain decision making and portfolio management of ideas.

However, creating smaller and thus more ideas to pushed through the funnel means that the management attention per idea spreads thinner, not in the least because the budget per idea becomes smaller and managers are understandably reluctant to spend their valuable time on such small investments. To make matters worse, a higher flow of ideas through the funnel demands management attention more frequently.

The natural response of organizations might be to optimize the time of management by grouping ideas into bigger budget requests and by reducing the frequency of innovation governance board meetings. Although such efficiency may save valuable management time, it also decreases flow. It is not difficult to calculate that the value represented by an increased flow of innovations vastly outweighs the time saved by managers.

The solution to the problem is not to increase the number of managers. The primary skill of management in the process of innovation is to elaborate on the long term, strategic value potential of individual innovations. Not all ideas in the funnel require this management skill at each stage of their development. Flow can be greatly optimized if part of the portfolio management activities can be mandated by management to the innovation coaches. This mandate can include smaller budget or resource allocations, decisions about moving from the validation to the experimentation phase. The innovation coaches work as an extension of the innovation governance board with a clear goal to optimize flow of ideas and allowing management to focus attention on where it truly adds value.

On many assignments with clients, I have come across objections to the role of innovators and innovation coaches. Such objections often state that the innovation process is too heavy, requiring too many people and more segregated budget lines. Many people claim that the existing organization should be able to handle something as straight forward as the innovation process.

My answer is clear: the existing process in organizations is aimed at achieving maximum efficiency at running the current business. By design, that means that innovations are seen as inefficient, and any attention given to them as 'a distraction from what is really important.' This leads to lack of attention, slow decision making and poor output. Such poor management of innovations also slows down progress, both in flow of innovation *and* in the running organization. Yet, innovation cannot be separated from the running organization. It requires the ideas, skills, and time of employees from the current business in order to create the new. The continuous innovation process has the objective to use the time and resources from the existing organization as efficiently as possible to determine the potential value of ideas as quickly as possible. The time saved in the organization always outweighs the time invested by coaches. But the real value from the process lies in the increased speed of delivery of ideas to market. That is why the speed of flow of ideas through an organization is the best measure for success.

Epilogue

How Gales of Creative Destruction have become a steady wind of change

When Schumpeter described his theory of Gales of Creative Destruction, he went out of his way to explain that "in dealing with capitalism we are dealing with an evolutionary process" (Schumpeter, 1942). However, rather than accrediting this change to generic social and economic changes, such as revolution, war and population or capital increase, Schumpeter shows us that "the fundamental impulse that sets and keeps the capitalist engine in motion comes from the new customer goods, the new methods for production and transportation, the new markets, the new forms of industrial organization that capitalist enterprise creates." Schumpeter then argues that, when analyzing economic principles, scientists tend to take make the mistake of using the status quo as a point of reference to explain current events and corporate strategies. "…the problem that is usually being visualized is how corporations administers existing structures, whereas the relevant problem is how it creates and destroys them."

Schumpeter's notion of economic change drivers is that of innovative products, production technologies, logistics, and organizational structures. Even though his own (early) life was awash with turmoil and change, Schumpeter's world was a far cry from today's fast-paced, digital environment. A world in which business cycles have shrunk to singular points, in which the difference between exploitation and exploration has seized to exist and in which the time between sense and respond has become zero. Today, reverting back to his insight, with a good degree of freedom of interpretation, we could conclude that: "...the problem that is usually being visualized is how capitalism administers existing structures, whereas the relevant problem is how continuous innovation creates and destroys them." Through digitization and datafication, Schumpeter's 'Gales of Creative Destruction' has become a steady wind of change, a steady flow of Continuous Innovation.

Join our community

Innovation Requires Inspiration

The Continuous Innovation Framework, (COIN) is a publicly available, open framework. It is a blueprint for an organizational model to foster Continuous Innovation. COIN consists of

- A free and open Body of Knowledge, available at http://www.continuousinnovation.net
- A community of experts on LinkedIn.com (Group: COIN - Continuous Innovation Framework), organizing regular meet-ups and round table discussions around the world
- Training and certification for all levels of innovation specialists and senior management

Feel free to join the community today and visit http://www.continuousinnovation.net

Bibliography

Ajaz, A. a. (2012). *Velocity, The Seven New Laws For a World Gone Digital.* London: Random House.

Albertson, M. (2017, July 14). *Caterpillar's story of connecting half a million machines.* Retrieved November 27, 2017, from Silicon Angle: https://siliconangle.com/blog/2017/07/14/caterpillar-plans-to-connect-half-a-million-machines-subscribed17/

Aronowitz, S. a. (2015, 06). *Getting Organizational Redesign Right.* Retrieved from McKinsey.com: https://www.mckinsey.com/business-functions/organization/our-insights/getting-organizational-redesign-right

Baghai, M. C. (1999). *The Alchemy of Growth.* New York: Perseus Publishing.

Bielaszka-DuVernay, C. (2009, 1). *Broadening the Brand.* Retrieved from Harvard Business Review: https://hbr.org/2009/01/broadening-the-brand

Brynjolfsson, E. a. (2016). *The Second Machine Age: Work, Progress and Prosperity in a Time of Brilliant Technologies.* W.W. Norton & Co.

CB Insights Inc. (2014). *The R.I.P. Report – Startup Death Trends.* Retrieved 03 20, 2016, from CB Insights: https://www.cbinsights.com/blog/startup-death-data/

Christensen, C. M. (1995). Disruptive Technologies Catching the Wave. *Harvard Business Review*, p. 3.

Christensen, C. M. (1997). *The Innovator's Dilemma.* Harvard Business School Press.

Christensen, C. M. (2015). *What is Disruptive Innovation.* Retrieved 05 18, 2016, from Harvard Business Review: https://hbr.org/2015/12/what-is-disruptive-innovation#

Diamandis, P. a. (2012). *Abundance: The Future Is Better Than You Think.* Free Press.

Diamandis, P. a. (2015). *Bold: How to Go Big, Create Wealth and Impact the World.* Simon & Schuster.

Fitzgerald, M. (2016, 4 29). *General Motors Relies on IoT to Anticipate Customers' Needs.* Retrieved 5 5, 2016, from MIT Sloan Management REVIEW: http://sloanreview.mit.edu/article/general-motors-relies-on-iot-to-keep-its-customers-safe-and-secure/

Ford, M. (2015). *Rise of the Robots: Technology and the Threat of a Jobless Future.* Oneworld Publications.

Fortune Magazine. (2016, 01 26). *Here's Why Xerox Is Splitting up | Fortune.* Retrieved 07 24, 2017, from YouTube.com: https://www.youtube.com/watch?v=wH1-J9Y5MC8

Gladwell, M. (2000). *The Tipping Point: How Little Things Can Make a Big Difference.* Boston: Little, Brown.

Goodwin, T. (2015, 03 3). *The Battle Is For The Customer Interface.* Retrieved from TechCrunch.com: http://techcrunch.com/2015/03/03/in-the-age-of-disintermediation-the-battle-is-all-for-the-customer-interface

Gunther McGrath, R. a. (2000). *The Entrepreneurial Mindset: Strategies for Continuously Creating Opportunity in an Age of Uncertainty.* Boston: Harvard Business School Press.

Indvik, L. (2013, 04 02). *The 'Financial Times' Has a Secret Weapon: Data*. Retrieved 10 27, 2017, from Mashable.com: http://mashable.com/2013/04/02/financial-times-john-ridding-strategy/#F8yi0o.DLuq4

Jackson, J. (2014, 03 03). *Financial Times CEO: 'We've now achieved critical mass in digital'*. Retrieved 10 27, 2017, from The Media Briefing: https://www.themediabriefing.com/article/financial-times-pearson-john-ridding-subscriptions-digital-mobile

Kelly, K. (2010). *What Technology Wants*. Viking Press.

Kopalle, P. (2014, 01 28). *Why Amazons Anticipatory Shipping is Pure Genius*. Retrieved 01 14, 2018, from Forbes.com: https://www.forbes.com/sites/onmarketing/2014/01/28/why-amazons-anticipatory-shipping-is-pure-genius

Kurzweil, R. (2005). *The Singularity Is Near*. Viking.

Lapsley, P. (2011, 01 08). *The Greatest Bad Business Decision Quotation That Never Was*. Retrieved 11 16, 2016, from The History of Phone Phreaking: http://blog.historyofphonephreaking.org/2011/01/the-greatest-bad-business-decision-quotation-that-never-was.html

Mayer-Schoenberger, V. a. (2013). *Big Data: A Revolution That Will Transform How We Live, Work, and Think*. Eamon Dolan/Houghton Mifflin Harcourt.

Nagji, B. a. (2012, May). Managing Your Innovation Portfolio. *Harvard Business Review*.

O'Reilly, C. a. (2013, May 11). Organizational Ambidexterity: Past, Present and Future. Stanford, CA, USA.

O'Reilly, C. A. (2013). *Organizational Ambidexterity: Past, Present and Future.* Stanford: Academy of Management Perspectives.

Osterwalder, A. a. (2015). *Vale Proposition Design: How to Create Products and Services Customers Want.* Wiley and sons.

Porter, M. (2014, 11). *How Smart, Connected Products Are Transforming Competition.* Retrieved from Harvard Business Review: https://hbr.org/2014/11/how-smart-connected-products-are-transforming-competition

Ries, E. (2011). *The lean startup: How today's entrepreneurs use continuous innovation to create radically successful businesses.* USA: Crown Publishing Inc.

Ries, E. (2017, 07). *The Startup Way: How Modern Companies Use Entrepreneurial Management to Transform Culture and Drive Long-Term Growth.* Currency - The Crown Publishing Group.

Rogers, E. (1962). *Diffusion of Innovations.* USA: Glencoe: Free Press.

Satell, G. (2014, 09 05). *A Look Back At Why Blockbuster Really Failed And Why It Didn't Have To.* Retrieved 02 27, 2017, from Forbes.com: https://www.forbes.com/sites/gregsatell/2014/09/05/a-look-back-at-why-blockbuster-really-failed-and-why-it-didnt-have-to

Scaled Agile Inc. (2019, 04 20). *Agile Architecture.* Retrieved from Scaled Agile Framework: https://www.scaledagileframework.com/agile-architecture/

Schumpeter, J. (1942). *Capitalism, Socialism and Democracy.* New York: Harper & Brothers.

Slocum Jensen, L. (2016, 04 1). *Connected Cars Landschap 2016.*
Retrieved 01 20, 2017, from Venture Beat:
https://www.vbprofiles.com/l/connectedcarstwitter

Spijker, A. v. (2014). *The New Oil: Using Innovative Business Models
to Turn Data Into Profit.* New York: Technics Publications.

Startup Genome. (2016). Retrieved 03 07, 2017, from The Startup
Genome: http://startupgenome.com/

Svahn, F. M. (2017). Embracing Digital Innovation in Incumbent
Firms: How Volvo Cars Managed Competing Concerns. *MIS
Quarterly Vol. 41 No. 1*, 239 - 253.

Taleb, N. (2012). *Antifragile: Things That Gain from Disorder.*
Random House.

The Darwin Correspondence Project. (n.d.). *Six things Darwin never
said – and one he did.* Retrieved 2013 йил 23-09 from The
Darwin Correspondence Project:
http://www.darwinproject.ac.uk/six-things-darwin-never-said

Viereckl, R. a. (2016). *Connected Car Report 2016.* PWC Strategy&.
PWC Strategy&.

West, G. (2017). *Scale: The Universal Laws of Growth, Innovation,
Sustainability and the Pace of Life in Organisms, Cities,
Economies, and Companies.* New York: Penguin.

Wong, J. C. (2016, 01 21). *Seattle bookstores face new threat from
Amazon: a brick-and-mortar location.* Retrieved 03 01, 2017,
from The Guardian:
https://www.theguardian.com/technology/2016/jan/21/amazon
-books-opens-seattle-independent-bookstores

Yoskovitz, B. a. (2013). *Lean Analytics: Use Data to Build a Better
Startup Faster.* O'Reilly.

Index

www.ingramcontent.com/pod-product-compliance
Lightning Source LLC
Chambersburg PA
CBHW071104050326
40690CB00008B/1105

9 781634 625623